An Introduction to Powerboat Cruising

An Introduction to Powerboat Cruising

DAG PIKE

HEARST MARINE BOOKS
New York

Contents

Introduction

It was 40 years ago that I made my first voyage in a motor cruiser. The voyage was notable because we went aground coming into harbour and had to be towed off, the only damage being to the skipper's pride. I was too young to care at the time, but I think we all learned something from that grounding. That learning continued over the next 40 years, and I hope that I can pass some of it on in this book.

There are so many facets to handling and looking after a motor cruiser and most of them are learned by experience. Each time you go on board or go off to sea there will be something new to cope with, but quite quickly you will become comfortable with the boat and in tune with the sea which will allow you to get the maximum fun and experience from your boat.

One of your first problems when you take over the boat will usually be that you are in a crowded marina. This is not the place to learn boat handling and you would be wise to ask someone to help you out to sea the first time, so that you don't have to make embarrassing mistakes in front of other owners.

Out in the open sea there is much more room to manoeuvre and you can practise away from damaging habour walls and get the feel of the sea and the way the boat responds to it. You do have to get back into harbour again, which can be difficult as things tend to crowd in on you the nearer you get to your berth.

Having someone experienced with you on these early outings is a help, but you will only really learn when you have to do it on your own. When this moment comes, work it all out carefully beforehand so that you don't get any nasty surprises, take your time, and you will soon find that it is not nearly as difficult as you imagined. It may help to wait until slack water to reduce the number of factors you have to consider.

Handling the boat is just one facet of motor cruising. There is a lot to learn about the weather, about the sea and about navigation. You don't have to grasp these all at once; instead, take your time, choose the conditions and places where you go to sea so that initially you only have good conditions and easy navigation, then gradually you can extend the limits as you gain confidence. Even when you are very experienced, it's a good idea to always keep something in reserve so that if things do go wrong (and they will on even the best organised boat), you should be able to cope.

Much of this ability to cope will come from knowing your boat well. If you are an average owner you will spend a great deal of your time on board in harbour. Here you can still continue the learning process by finding out everything you can about the boat. How are the steering systems routed? What makes the electrical system tick? How does the plumbing work? Boats and their systems can be quite complex and the more you know about them the better you will cope.

It sounds almost like going back to school, but this learning can be done in your own time and at your own pace. Look at other boats and how people handle them, and be aware of the ever changing sea and weather. In no time at all you will be handling situations like a professional and you'll get the rewards and satisfaction that come with it. Hopefully, this book and the experience that has gone into it will help you along the road to becoming an experienced and competent motor cruiser owner and handler.

1 · The boat

HULLS

As the proud owner of a motor cruiser, you will admire your boat mainly for the sections above water. However, it is the underwater sections which really count in terms of performance and as a starting point towards getting to know your boat you need to understand something of the world of motor cruiser hull design.

In the motor cruiser world a great deal is talked about hull design as though having a particular form of hull is a magic formula towards producing the perfect craft. Hull design is important because the hull is the part of the boat which comes in direct contact with the water and the shape needs to be right if the boat is to have good performance and handling characteristics. However, there is no special secret to hull design – although the merits of one designer's work compared with another's is often a discussion point amongst boat owners. It is as though the designer's work stops once he has designed the hull, but nothing could be further from the truth. The designer's job is to produce a fully integrated motor cruiser with a hull which performs well in the appropriate conditions, with comfortable accommodation, well laid out controls and the right machinery to give the boat its desired performance.

The two main types of hull form for motor cruisers are planing and displacement. Perhaps we should add a third type – the semi-displacement hull. As its name implies, this is a sort of halfway house between the other two.

To a certain extent the type of hull which a motor cruiser has dictates its speed capabilities, but all hulls must be operable at slow speeds, so there are certain common factors in hull designs. Even craft that have engines which make them only capable of displacement speeds often have planing hulls, which illustrates the intimate interchange in hull types, although there is no question of using a displacement hull at anything above displacement speeds.

The Displacement Hull
The term 'displacement hull' speaks for itself. The hull is supported in the water by the weight and volume of the water which the hull displaces. If you remember Archimedes' Law from your schooldays you will know that any floating object displaces an amount of water equal to its own weight. Any boat at rest obeys this law but a displacement boat also obeys it when it is

A Dutch built steel cruiser offers a comfortable and practical solution to motor cruising at displacement speeds. (Photo: Linssen)

moving. As the boat moves forward the water is displaced and flows back to fill the gap at the stern as the boat passes.

This movement of water out from the bow and in at the stern creates a wave form which is related to the length of the boat. At moderate speeds of around 6 or 7 knots the displacement motor cruiser moves very comfortably in this wave form. However, once the speed is increased above this range the hull starts to meet a lot of resistance. This is because the hull is trying to raise itself up and overtake the wave it has created but there is insufficient lift in the hull shape to allow it to do so. Effectively, if you put too much power into this type of hull, all that happens is that the stern squats and the bow lifts and the boat will go along at an uncomfortable angle but will not go a great deal faster.

The length of the wave generated by a displacement hull is very much related to the length of the hull. Longer boats will generally be able to travel at higher speeds than shorter ones. For a motor cruiser around 30 feet in length, 6 to 7 knots is likely to be a comfortable speed, and the maximum speed will be in the region of 8 to 9 knots. Because of the almost brick wall-like resistance resulting from the wave form generated by the hull, increasing the speed of a displacement hull from, say, 6 to 8 knots will probably require twice the amount of power as that required to get the boat running up to 6 knots. The fuel consumption will also increase dramatically and the boat will make a lot of fuss with very little effect in terms of performance. Used intelligently, a displacement boat can give a very economical performance; this means keeping the speed down to a level at which the boat operates comfortably. You can soon tell when you are pushing a displacement hull too hard by the way the boat responds. All you are doing if you exceed a comfortable speed is burning much more fuel, with little benefit.

Displacement hulls can travel faster if they are very long and narrow and this was certainly the fashion sixty or seventy years ago before planing boats were fully developed. However, long narrow boats do not allow comfortable accommodation on board and a modern displacement hull has a well-rounded form with generous beam to give plenty of space inside. This form tends to make the hull comfortable at sea; the image of displacement hulls is one of sea-kindly boats proceeding at a leisurely pace.

Many modern displacement hulls follow the planing boat form with a hard chine hull (a design with a sharp angle where the bottom of the boat meets the sides). These hulls are cut off square at the stern with a flat transom and they can work surprisingly well at slow speeds provided they have been designed for the job. A full bow is generally required to balance the full stern shape, and a skeg, which is like a small keel, is often used to give directional stability and propeller protection if the boat has to sit on the bottom.

The Planing Hull
In contrast, planing hulls tend to be aggressive, with comfort

The fine lines of a modern sports cruiser where speed has priority in the design. (Photo: Colombo)

taking second place to performance. Whereas the displacement hull moves through the water a planing boat moves over it. Therefore, it is much more sensitive to the waves and rides accordingly. When power is applied to a planing hull, it first of all starts to move through the water in just the same way as a displacement hull, generating the wave form which builds up resistance. However, the underwater surfaces of a planing hull are shaped so that, when the water flowing past the hull strikes it, lift is generated. This lift raises the boat up in the water, thus overcoming the wave resistance and allowing the boat to travel on the surface at high speeds. In this condition the weight of the boat is supported mainly by the dynamic lift generated by the water flowing past and under the hull, with only a small proportion of the weight being supported by the water which is displaced.

In order to generate this dynamic lift the underwater surfaces of the hull have to be carefully shaped to run at the correct angle. Large flat surfaces which run at a very slight angle to the surface of the water enable the water striking them to generate lift without creating too much resistance. By using the flap or power trim controls on a planing boat you are, in fact, altering this angle of lift and, in doing so, raising or lowering the bow.

When a planing boat comes up on to the plane you may be conscious of a considerable change of trim (the boat's fore and aft angle in the water). This is because the boat is lifting up over the hull-generated wave as it comes onto the plane. On many early planing boat designs there was a very noticeable 'hump' as the boat came onto the plane but with modern design and more power this 'hump' is far less noticeable. Modern planing boats come onto the plane smoothly and easily, which is useful because it allows the boat to operate at slower speeds around this 'hump' speed in reasonable sea conditions.

Semi-displacement Hulls
The semi-displacement type hull also tends to operate in this 'hump' speed range, generally between 10 and 20 knots. These craft try to combine the virtues of displacement and planing hulls in one hybrid design.

The motive behind the semi-displacement hull is to create a

design which is equally effective at both low and high speeds. The hull design incorporates flat areas to generate lift but it also has rounded bilges and softer lines than those found on the typical planing boat giving a more seaworthy and softer ride. Semi-displacement boats tend to require greater power for a given speed than a pure planing boat. They also tend to make a bit of a fuss when they are travelling at speeds over 10 knots because they are not properly on the plane and yet not operating in the displacement mode either. There is a danger, because they fall between the two more conventional hull designs, that they do not always pick up the best attributes of either, and it takes very careful design to produce a successful semi-displacement hull.

With advances in planing boat design the demand for semi-displacement hulls is tending to disappear because a

A semi-displacement cruiser designed primarily for speeds in the 10–20 knot range. (Photo: Fjord Plast (UK) Ltd)

well-designed planing boat can operate at intermediate and displacement speeds just as well as a semi-displacement hull – although, as with most aspects of boat design, the margins between the different types of hull form are blurred.

Hull Shape and Seaworthiness
Seaworthiness is a factor which is hard to quantify in boat design. There is more discussion about this aspect than any other when boat owners get together. Seaworthiness, to a large degree, is dependent on the shape of the hull. However, other factors, such as the power and propulsion system and the controls, also have a considerable bearing on seaworthiness. It is not always possible, therefore, to isolate hull design as the sole influence.

Seaworthiness can usually be described as the way the hull accommodates itself to the wave patterns and, as we shall see in later chapters, a *good* seaworthy boat has to be capable not only of operating in a wide variety of wave types but also in seas coming from different directions. Quite often the requirements can be contradictory, so the boat designer finds he has to make a series of compromises to arrive at the optimum shape for any particular boat. Judging by some modern designs, seaworthiness is not always the top priority so, as a motor cruiser owner, you will need to have some idea of the capabilities of your boat. You will then know how far you can push it in different conditions.

Stern Shape
A seaworthy displacement hull shape is epitomised by the traditional lifeboat, with its double-ended hull shape and pronounced sheerline, i.e. the curve of the deckline, which rises at each end. These high ends to the boat give it plenty of buoyancy fore and aft when the boat has to lift to cope with head or following seas, and help to prevent waves breaking on board.

Few displacement motor cruiser hulls on the market today adopt these same seaworthy lines. The tendency is to have a square transom stern which gives much more space inside the hull. This compromises the seaworthiness to a certain extent but one has to remember that a lifeboat is designed for extreme sea conditions. When a designer sets out to produce a displacement motor cruiser hull he is considering a boat that will operate quite safely and comfortably in conditions up to about Force 6 winds. For this type of application the transom stern is quite adequate and gives you a lot more boat for your money. A large square transom would prove to be a bit of a handful in a big following sea, as later chapters will show.

Bow Shape
Matching the full stern shape provided by a transom stern should be a good full bow form so that the bow will lift readily to waves when running into a head sea. The bow shape is probably the most difficult area for compromise because if it is very full the response to oncoming waves will be too rapid, making the bow lift and fall over every wave and resulting in a fairly violent pitching motion. Make the bow finer and initially it will cut through the wave before the buoyancy starts to take effect and

A double-ended displacement cruiser which owes its origins to lifeboat and fishing boat designs. (Photo: Windy Boats)

the lift starts. Fine the bow away too much and there is not sufficient buoyancy for the bow to lift readily and the hull then ploughs through the waves, possibly shipping water. The fullness of the bow has considerable bearing on the seaworthiness of the boat when operating in a head sea. Introduce a flare into the bow and the designer can then combine a fine entry in the lower sections with a wider, fuller shape higher up. This is a good compromise and is the favoured bow shape on many displacement hulls.

The shape of the bow also determines whether the boat is wet or dry. On a wet boat, the bow will generate a lot of spray which will curl up over the decks and make life uncomfortable. A dry boat will have the spray firmly under control, tending to turn it downwards and away from the deck. It's all a question of bow shape, the sweep of the chine line (the angle where the bottom and the sides of the hull meet) and the spray rails.

Bilge Shape
The next factor we need to consider with regard to seaworthy hull shape is the bilges, where the sides of the boat turn into the bottom. A sharp angle or a barely rounded shape here results in what might be considered a hard hull form. Such a hull will respond quite sharply to beam seas (i.e. those approaching from the side) because of the sudden change of shape at the bilge, resulting in quite a sharp rolling motion. A more rounded bilge will give a more comfortable motion in a beam sea. The underwater shape of the hull should be measured against the transverse stability and the position of the centre of gravity of the boat — a boat with a low centre of gravity will be very stable but it will also tend to roll quite sharply, whereas if the centre of gravity is higher up you will get an easier more gentle roll but the hull will also be less stable.

To a certain extent you can determine the stability characteristics of a boat when you step aboard. If it hardly moves as you step onto the side then it is a hard boat that will probably give you quite an uncomfortable ride. If it tips to a certain extent when you come on board then it will probably have a softer motion. To many people this seems contradictory. They feel that a boat which is 'tippy' in harbour will not be safe at sea but, in fact, you will usually find that the 'tippy' boat is more comfortable.

Planing Hull Shapes

With planing boats many of the factors concerned with seaworthiness apply even though the boat is riding on the surface rather than in the water. A fine bow entry is necessary when working in a head sea to reduce the lift at the bow and to enable it to cut through the waves. A full bow will cause the boat to lift out of the water and 'fly'. The deep vee hull, which is now almost universally used on planing motor cruisers, is a compromise between the most efficient planing form – which is a flat-bottomed hull – and the need to impart a cushioning effect into the hull when it hits waves. By introducing the vee into the bottom sections of the hull this cushioning effect is achieved and if this is combined with a fine entry at the bow then you have a boat which will perform well in head seas.

A fine example of a deep vee hull which is derived from offshore racing designs. (Photo: Cougar Marine)

However, a good head sea performance is not the only consideration. A designer must also produce a hull design which will work well in a following sea, when the bow needs to have plenty of buoyancy. This demands a fuller shape. Hence a designer must compromise, and again a flare is often introduced into the bow section. This means that, although the initial entry is fairly fine, the bow widens out quite considerably above the water line, giving the buoyancy necessary to provide lift as the bow starts to become immersed in a wave.

The transom stern found on all planing boats is essential because this sharp cutaway allows the water to peel off from the hull when the boat is on the plane. As we have seen, the transom stern is not the ideal shape in a following sea at displacement speeds but at planing speeds it works well because the boat is overtaking the following seas, which means there is no risk of the following waves impacting on the large flat surface of the transom. Planing boats do have to operate at displacement speeds at times, however, and in these circumstances a large transom can make for an uncomfortable ride. The sea hitting the transom can have a significant effect on the steering, particularly if you only have small rudders which are common on planing boats.

Another point to bear in mind with a planing craft is that when the boat is on the plane the bow lifts up when speed increases, allowing the boat to run at a suitable angle to meet oncoming waves. When the boat comes off the plane and operates at displacement speed the bow can drop quite significantly. This reduces the freeboard, producing a risk of the bow burying into waves at these slower speeds particularly when operating in short steep seas. Planing boats often have a reverse sheer on the deckline so that the deck is highest in the middle and drops away at each end, which can increase the risk of seas breaking on board at slow speeds. A recent trend is to have an almost straight deckline which helps to increase the freeboard at the bow. In most cases modern motor cruisers have a hull shape in which designers have managed to match the requirements of high and low speed performance adequately.

You can't do a great deal to change the shape of your boat's hull once you have bought it, but understanding how the shape responds to waves can help you to drive the boat more intelligently. The basic rule to remember is that if your boat has a fine hull shape then it will respond less positively to waves whereas a very full hull shape will respond very quickly. To a certain extent these effects can be counteracted or enhanced by the use of flaps or power trim (see Chapter 2). Even the throttle can have an effect on the trim and so, particularly on a planing motor cruiser, there are a lot of tunes you can play to match the boat to different conditions. It is worth spending time on the water experimenting in moderate conditions to get a better feel for your boat. You will then be far better prepared if you find yourself caught out in bad weather, and you will be able to make the best use of your boat's seaworthy characteristics.

Skegs, Chines and Spray Rails
Once a designer has worked on the basic shape of the hull he can fine tune it by means of skegs, chines and spray rails. There is particular scope for this on planing hulls, where fine tuning not only helps to improve the seaworthiness and performance of the hull but can also be used to improve the steering.

The skeg is the fin on the bottom of the hull which terminates at the keel. On displacement boats it is usually cut away at the stern to form the propeller aperture, whilst on twin screw boats it stops short of the propellers. Skegs are not found on deep vee hulls.

The skeg helps to protect the propeller and rudder if the boat goes aground, but its main function is to balance the hull to give good steering. A boat will normally have good directional stability if it is deeper at the stern than the bow. If the right balance is achieved by means of the skeg then only a minimum of steering will be needed to keep the boat on a straight course.

A planing boat sometimes lacks directional stability at slow speeds, which can be very disconcerting when manoeuvring in harbour. Planing boats can change their trim quite considerably between slow and high speeds and the bow invariably drops down at slower speeds. This upsets the steering balance so that when you turn the wheel the boat tends to sheer off quite suddenly. This problem can be reduced by moving fuel, water or any other moveable weight further aft. An alternative is to give the boat a little more throttle, which will lift the bow sufficiently to restore directional stability.

The angle at which the bottom of the boat meets the side is called the chine on a planing hull. Seen in profile, if the line of the chine keeps low, running almost parallel to the water, then the boat tends to have a full bow shape. If the line of the chine curves up forward almost to deck level then the boat will have a finer bow shape and this is usually matched to a steeply raking stem. Faster boats tend to have the latter shape whilst slower and displacement boats have the lower line. Of course, on many displacement boats there is no chine line because the hull sides curve gracefully into the hull bottom in what is termed a round bilge.

Spray rails are narrow horizontal surfaces added to the hull bottoms of planing boats to generate lift, to give stability and to

Spray rails in action, peeling the water away from the hull and reducing the wetted area. (Photo: Italmarine)

reduce the wetted surface area of the hull. They are triangular in cross-section and run fore and aft. Designers of planing motor cruisers have differing views about spray rails. In some cases spray rails are only applied at the fore part of the hull where they help to peel away the water from the hull, reducing the area in contact with the water and thus the resistance. In other cases the spray rails run all the way aft and here the designer is using the rails to generate extra lift and to give better directional stability. A similar flat surface is also introduced under the chine to help generate lift. This chine rail is often quite wide and is sometimes angled down. When using spray rails and chines the designer is striving to achieve a balanced hull which will come onto the plane easily and have good directional stability. He must resist the temptation to make the rails and chine too wide, otherwise there will be slamming when the sea hits the flat surfaces.

GOOD BOATS AND BAD BOATS

With all this emphasis on hull design, performance and style, how do you tell a good boat from a bad boat? You may try a boat at sea and not feel particularly happy about it, whilst the salesman is trying to convince you that it is a good boat and ideal for your purpose. Conversely, what you think is a good boat on first acquaintance may turn out to be something of a disap- pointment when you get to know it better. So, what *are* the characteristics of a good boat?

If there was a simple answer to that question there probably wouldn't be any bad boats on the market. A good boat is a combination of many qualities but at the end of the day it is not just the boat which has to be judged but also the person driving it. You may be unhappy with the way the controls are laid out. They may be difficult to operate smoothly and cohesively and therefore you will not be able to drive the boat in the way the designer intended. Alternatively, you may have a boat which is designed specifically for fine weather and which has an emphasis on luxury. If you take this boat out and try using it in bad sea conditions you may find it wanting.

Boat builders often offer a complete range of engines, from very low to very high power. Choosing an engine at either extreme of this range may mean that your boat will not perform well. A low-powered engine could mean that your boat rides at the wrong trim, perhaps behaving like a semi-displacement boat rather than a planing hull. A high-powered engine could mean that your boat becomes quite a handful because the engine is pushing it beyond its capabilities. There are many factors which may influence your decision about whether a boat is right for you, most of them subjective. On their own certain features may not be bad, but compounded with other features you may end up with something that is not particularly good.

Balance
What you are really looking for in a motor cruiser is balance and this is difficult to define. As far as hull design is concerned the balance comes from having nothing too extreme in the hull form. If you visit a boat show you find that the popular motor cruisers are in the middle of the range as far as hull form is concerned. Anything with extremes of hull design, such as trihedrals or even catamarans, can offer benefits in particular areas of motor cruising, but if you want a good all round boat then you should go for a middle-of-the-road design. You want a nicely balanced hull with a moderate bow which looks as though it will take kindly to the waves coming from ahead or astern; a transom which is neither too big nor too bulky; and amidship sections which are not too harsh and angular but which look as though they will have a comfortable affinity with the waves.

If high performance is your yardstick then you will be looking for a leaner, hungrier type of hull, perhaps narrower in the beam and finer at the bow. If 20 knots is your favourite cruising speed, however, then a much beamier, fuller hull design will suit your requirements. The lightweight, high-strength hulls required for high performance are invariably over-designed for use at lower speeds. Indeed, the extra weight of a good, solid hull used for low speed motor cruising can provide you with a great deal more comfort and a welcome feeling of security, which is often lacking in a lightweight, high speed hull.

Looking at a boat at a show is one thing but you should also see it on the water and take it out and run it at different speeds to get a real feel for it. But even so you can't isolate hull design from all the other factors: the engine power has to match the hull and the steering capabilities have to match the speed, whilst the controls and seating at the control position have to match the driver and the performance. Hull design is thus only one of many factors to be judged in assessing the qualities of a motor cruiser. There is no doubting that it is an important factor and it is one which will have a considerable bearing on the handling and performance of the boat, particularly in waves.

CONSTRUCTION AND MAINTENANCE

Plastics
The vast majority of motor cruisers on the water today are constructed in glass-reinforced plastics (fiberglass), a most unlikely material for boat building, but one which has been developed since the 1950s into its present, highly sophisticated state. It comprises sheets of glass fiber filament which are impregnated with resin and laid up in a female mould. The hull is built up from successive layers until it reaches the designed thickness. After stiffening with stringers, and frames and bulkheads have been added, the hull is removed from the mould and then fitted out. One of the main attractions of using fiberglass is that because the mould has a very high surface finish the hull itself, when removed from the mould, has a similar very high quality finish. This finish, called the gel coat, is virtually impervious to the elements and will retain its finish for many years. Not only does this gel coat make the boat look attractive but it also reduces the maintenance required on the hull to the level of mainly cleaning it when the hull gets dirty.

With the improved quality of the glass fibers used for hull construction and the different types of resin such as epoxy and polyester used in the lay up the chemistry of fiberglass construction has improved greatly in recent years. In the early days there were many 'diseases' which afflicted these so-called plastic hulls and even recently blisters have attacked some fiberglass hulls and required major repair work to eradicate the problem. However, given a sound construction under the right conditions and strict quality control, a fiberglass hull can be built to last for many, many years with few problems for the owner.

There are many different fiberglass building methods used by manufacturers. In many cases the hull is built up simply with a solid laminate which is then stiffened internally by framing. This framing is built up using the same laminate which is formed over foam cores to create a girder-like structure to stiffen the hull. Both longitudinal and transverse stiffeners are employed in this way, the object being to reduce the panel size of the fiberglass structure and thus give it adequate strength and stiffness. Stiffness can also be achieved by using sandwich construction whereby, after the outside skin of the laminate has been laid up in the mould, a core of a special foam or balsa wood is laid on top of the laminate and then a further skin of laminate is laid up inside this to complete the structure. This sandwich or core construction produces an overall thicker laminate which has good insulating properties to reduce the effects of condensation. Sandwich construction also has sound deadening properties and is stiffer than a conventional laminate, which reduces or obviates the need for internal stiffening. However, to be successful, sandwich construction must have a positive bond between the two laminate skins on either side of the core and it requires careful design and building to produce a hull with the right characteristics.

Whilst only a proportion of motor cruiser builders use sandwich construction for the hull a great many more use the same type of construction for the superstructure. This is a less highly stressed area of the boat, but the insulating and stiffening qualities of sandwich construction can still be used to good effect.

Aluminium and Steel
Both aluminium and steel are used for motor cruiser construction. Aluminium is mainly used for planing craft where weight becomes more critical, whilst steel construction

is generally reserved for displacement craft and is growing in popularity in some countries.

Steel construction is generally cheaper than using other materials but it is prone to corrosion and needs careful preparation and painting if maintenance costs are to be kept down. It is not always easy to achieve the same high standard of finish with steel and aluminium as it is with fiberglass hulls unless filler is applied to the hull and long hours are spent rubbing this down to achieve a good surface finish before painting. If this has to be done the construction cost is usually somewhere close to that for fiberglass.

Aluminium is good for lightweight hulls although its use for motor cruiser construction is comparatively rare because it has little to offer in comparison with sophisticated fiberglass construction. Its use tends to be limited to one-off construction where the cost of a mould cannot be justified. Aluminium does offer benefits in terms of reduced maintenance but on the other hand considerable care has to be taken to prevent electrolytic corrosion on the hull structure. This occurs when different metals are used in the hull and its fittings, for example when bronze propellers are fitted to an aluminium hull. This combination generates electrolytic action in which the aluminium will be corroded unless special sacrificial anodes are fitted. The same thing can happen with steel hulls but the reaction is generally less severe.

Other Materials
Approximately 95 per cent of motor cruisers worldwide are constructed in fiberglass and there is no reason to expect this proportion to change dramatically in the next few years. As the chemistry of fiberglass construction becomes more advanced the standard of hulls and their longevity is likely to improve; some manufacturers of high performance motor cruisers are looking to use more exotic materials in the lay up for the hull structure. Materials like Kevlar and carbon fiber can increase the strength of a laminate considerably, allowing a reduction in the weight of the structure. Such materials are mainly used in the construction of high performance boats.

The use of high performance laminates incorporating these materials is often used by salesmen to promote their boats but in many cases Kevlar and carbon fiber are incorporated when their use is not really justified. The saving in weight or the increase in strength may be quite small and does add to the cost. The use of these exotic fibers in the laminate also needs to be very carefully engineered. Their use is only justified where a high strength lightweight craft is required.

MAINTENANCE

Although fiberglass is largely a maintenance free material it does require inspection on at least an annual basis to make sure that there has been no deterioration. On the outside of the hull this inspection should largely be to identify areas where the gel coat has been chipped or scratched, perhaps through impact when coming alongside. A thorough inspection of the surface should also detect any other imperfections in the gel coat such as blisters (which might indicate trouble in the laminate underneath). All chips, scratches and other defects should be carefully ground out, dried thoroughly and then the area filled with gel coat. If the grinding out has involved cutting through some of the layers of laminate underneath new material should be laid up into the hollow before a gel coat is applied. The gel coat will have to be sanded down using progressively finer sanding discs until the area can be polished smooth to blend into the existing gel coat. (Gel coat in the appropriate colours can normally be obtained from the original boat builder.)

The underwater areas should be cleaned to remove all marine growth and new anti-fouling paint will probably be required on an annual basis although in some waters it is possible to extend the period to two years where marine growth is not too serious a problem. The hull should also be thoroughly inspected on the inside and where wood is bonded into the structure in the form of bulkheads, stiffeners or support for interior fittings. This timber should then be closely inspected to make sure that no rot has started, which is possible if water has been allowed to lie in proximity to it. Where you can get access to the interior of the hull laminate you should check that there are no signs of delamination. If you have suffered any particularly strong impacts on the hull during the year the laminate inside should be inspected here for any signs of cracks or other damage. If found, these should be treated by a professional boat builder.

Such checks ensure that all is in order but should also identify any potential trouble spots long before they become serious. The annual maintenance check should also include an inspection of all skin fittings, making sure that they are still securely fastened, that there are no signs of leaks and that all the associated pipework is in good condition. Look particularly at the securing clips for the pipework. At the same time check that all the seacocks work efficiently. This sort of inspection is not only a good precaution against future trouble but also enables you to get to know your boat. The more familiar you are with your boat the more likely you are to be able to cope with any problems which might arise at sea.

2 · Controlling your motor cruiser

PRACTICE MAKES PERFECT

A crowded marina is not the place to learn boat handling. Your insurance company will not thank you if you gain your first experience of motor cruiser handling in crowded waters with expensive boats close alongside and with unforgiving quays and jetties.

A much safer (and less embarrassing) place to practise is out at sea. Find a quiet stretch of calmish water where you will be able to see the effect on the boat when you experiment with the throttles and steering. At this stage forget about the flaps and power trim (if your boat is fitted with them). Instead, concentrate on the throttles and steering because these are the two controls which you will use going in and out of harbour. Practise using these controls in open water and you will feel much more confident in the confined waters of a marina.

If you have a single propeller boat take note of the effects of steering the boat both with the propeller turning and with the propeller stopped. Notice also the effect on the steering when you put the engine into gear with the rudder hard over to one side. Try the engine astern and see how effective the steering is when running in this direction.

On a twin screw boat there are more controls to play with so in addition to the above you can try one engine ahead and one engine astern to see how the boat turns. While you are doing this see what effect turning the steering wheel from one side to the other has. Try running the boat ahead on one engine and see if you can steer the boat in a straight line, and then see what effect this has when you turn the boat in either direction. Finally try steering the boat astern in a straight line using both the rudder and the engine controls to maintain the course.

Experimenting with the controls in this way will give you a grounding in how to manoeuvre your boat in different circumstances. However, out at sea there are no fixed reference points so you will not see the effect of the more subtle manoeuvres which are required when coming alongside. The next stage in your training programme should be to find a convenient buoy (preferably not a navigation mark!) for use as a fixed reference point and practise manoeuvring the boat in its vicinity. Try practising when there is a tide running (either in or out) so that you can experience its effect. First of all come up towards the buoy against the tide and try holding the boat in position at a fixed distance downstream from it. This will give you experience of the more subtle effects of holding a boat in position using both the steering and the engine controls. From here you can try holding the boat in position a little distance away from the buoy when it is alongside you. This is much more difficult because you don't have a reference point ahead to steer by. It will quickly become evident what a mess you can get into if you let the boat drift too far off the line of the tide by using too much helm. Once the boat drifts off in this way you will need a lot of helm and a lot of room to get yourself back in line with the tide. This will teach you to use the helm carefully when you are coming alongside when a tide is running. Once you have built up confidence you will find that you can move the boat in and out from the buoy under full control just as you should when going alongside.

Manoeuvring a boat in a tide is often much easier than trying to handle a boat when there is no tide running. With the tide running you can more or less hold the boat at a fixed point and still keep steerage control, but with no tide the boat lies dead in the water, you have no steering control and you will find that you have to use the engine thrust more. This brings us to the next stage in your boat handling practice, which is to throw a fender or other floating object over the side at sea and try to come alongside it. It is often much more difficult than you realise but it will add to your boat handling experience and is good practice should you ever be faced with a man overboard situation. A word of warning: use a fender without a rope attached for this exercise, otherwise you might find the rope becomes wrapped around your propellers if you make a mistake.

Your early practice should preferably be in conditions where there is very little wind. In time try the same manoeuvres when there is a fresh breeze to give you an insight into the effect of the wind on boat handling. You may be lucky and find the wind and the tide running in the same direction, in which case boat handling is fairly straightforward. But if the wind is on the beam or against the tide you may find yourself in difficulties as you try to balance one against the other. This is where skill in boat handling really begins to tell, and in a fresh breeze even experienced boat handlers can find themselves in trouble manoeuvring at close quarters. Manoeuvring alongside a floating object when there is a wind blowing can, in fact, be easy because the wind acts rather like the tide in this situation, and if you put the bow into the wind you need just a little power to hold yourself in a fixed position. To reiterate, practice in all sorts of different situations out at sea is what is required, then you can begin to move into more difficult situations.

The next stage is to find a barge or unused jetty where you can practise going alongside – somewhere out of sight of onlookers is always a good idea. Put out plenty of fenders so that when you make mistakes, as you almost certainly will in the early stages, these won't result in damage to the boat. Try going alongside with the bow into the tide and with the stern into the tide just to appreciate the differences involved. Then repeat this exercise when there is some wind to make life more difficult; this will help widen your experience. The more time you spend practising like this unobserved in an environment where making mistakes will not be a major catastrophe the more confident you will be to face the rigours of harbour manoeuvring, which we will look at in detail in Chapter 3.

THE CONTROLS

Now that you have developed a feel for your motor cruiser in the practice sessions it's time to learn more about the controls of the boat. Salesmen have a habit of simplifying things, and motor cruiser salesmen are apt to describe the handling of a motor boat as 'just like driving a motor car'. Nothing could be further from the truth, although when you sit behind the steering wheel of a motor cruiser the dashboard does bear a resemblance to that of a car. The comparison stops there. A car runs on a good positive surface and there is an instant response to the controls. Motor cruisers run on a surface which can at times be disconcertingly irregular, and can seem to have a mind of its own. The reaction to the controls can at times seem far from positive but this is where the skill comes in, and developing this skill can be fun when you understand what you are doing.

The first thing to do when you step aboard is to banish any ideas about car driving. This not only applies to the controls but also to the way the boat responds to the water. The wheels of a car only allow it to go backwards and forwards, but a boat can go sideways, too. It has a very tenuous grip on the water which the skilful boat handler can manipulate to produce the response he is looking for. You might cast envious eyes at owners who arrive in a marina and skilfully back their boats straight into berths without panic or fuss. All they are doing is first of all assessing the various influences which affect the boat and then using the controls to counteract them so that the boat arrives exactly where they wish.

Steering
There are two main methods of connecting the steering wheel to the rudder in modern motor cruisers. On smaller craft up to about 40 feet (12 metres) in length the power required to turn the rudder is comparatively small and so a simple mechanical or hydraulic link is used. For larger craft and for the higher powered stern drive units power-steering can become necessary because of the increased force required to turn the rudder. Power-steering systems usually operate with an engine-driven pump providing the hydraulic power. They can feel rather dead because there is very little feedback from the rudder. As a result the steering feels less 'sensitive' than a hand-steering system.

With mechanical systems the link between the steering wheel and the rudder is normally provided by a push/pull cable steering system which has a rack and pinion at the steering wheel to translate the rotary movement of the wheel into the push/pull motion. These mechanical systems are very reliable and require minimum maintenance. They are adequate for smaller boats but larger motor cruisers tend to opt for the hydraulic systems, either hand or engine pump-powered. All of these methods of steering can incorporate two station steering positions so that the boat can be operated from either the fly bridge or the main wheelhouse.

A motor cruiser's steering should be light and responsive without too many turns lock to lock; a comfortable system will have between one-and-a-half and two turns lock to lock. This is a good compromise between the quick response required for harbour manoeuvring and the sensitive steering required for maintaining a straight course at sea, when only small adjustments need to be made to the wheel. If the steering feels too heavy it can easily be made lighter by incorporating more turns lock to lock, but it can then become very hard work when

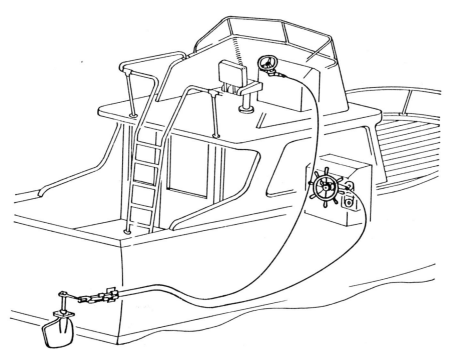

A typical two station steering layout using push-pull cables. Each wheel can be disconnected when not in use so that it doesn't turn.

you are manoeuvring in harbour. A better solution would be to incorporate some form of power assistance.

Modern steering systems are generally very reliable and require minimum maintenance. However, some boats have a form of emergency steering system as an added safety feature. This is usually an extension to the rudder spindle which comes up through the deck and has a squared end enabling a tiller to be fitted. With the steering system disconnected you have direct control of the rudder in case something breaks in the steering system itself. Since steering is such a vital component in controlling your boat the addition of an emergency steering system shows a sensible approach to safety. It is possible to rig up emergency steering systems by constructing a steering oar which can be lashed to the transom or by towing a strong bucket on one side or the other. These can serve to get you home if all else fails.

Rudders

The steering of the boat is actually performed by the rudder or rudders. On most twin propeller boats the rudders are located directly behind the propellers because the rudders work most effectively in the propeller slip stream. This is because the stream of water leaving the propeller is moving at greater speed than the water flowing past the boat. You will still be able to steer when the propeller is stopped but it is nothing like as efficient as when the propeller is turning. You will notice this difference when turning the boat if you suddenly open the throttle. Even before the boat's speed starts to increase there will be a noticeable increase in the rate at which the boat turns. You can use this steering thrust to good effect when manoeuvring at slow speeds in harbour.

The improved steering when you turn on the power is particularly noticeable on displacement boats, because they tend to have a larger rudder area than fast boats in order to achieve effective steering at the slower speeds at which they normally operate. Planing boats have a smaller rudder area to reduce resistance at high speeds. Although this rudder size is quite adequate to turn the boat at high speed, fast boats often lack good manoeuvrability at slow speeds. You must compensate for this by using the engine to assist steering.

The normal rudder used on motor cruisers today is the balanced type where part of the blade is forward of the pivot. When the rudder is turned at an angle to the water flow the pressure on the forward section of the blade helps to turn it, thus making the steering much lighter. However, the temptation to put too much area forward of the pivot should be resisted, otherwise the rudder does not self-centre easily and you find the boat over-steers and has poor directional stability.

Motor cruisers fitted with outboards or stern drives have no rudders. Steering works directly from the propulsion leg on the transom of the boat and the steering thrust is largely obtained by changing the angle at which the propeller drives. This gives a very positive steering action when the propeller is turning but when it is stopped you have only the narrow leg of the outboard or stern drive to act as a rudder which has only a limited steering effect. In Chapter 3 we shall see the differences between rudder and propeller steering and how they affect the handling of the boat in harbour. Out at sea they both feel much the same.

Flaps
Flaps are often referred to as trim tabs, but because of the possible confusion with the power trim used on stern drive and outboard propulsion systems I usually refer to them as 'flaps'. The flaps are hinged panels mounted on each side usually at the bottom outboard extremity of the transom. They have several functions. Used together they alter the boat's longitudinal trim, while used singly they level up the boat athwartships. When the flaps are hinged down under their hydraulic control cylinders the effect is to lift the stern of the boat, so putting it onto a more horizontal trim. With the flaps up the bow rises and the stern drops again.

By modifying the trim of the boat in this way you will find that you get a better angle of attack in waves, and this effect is particularly useful in keeping the bow down to reduce pounding when running into a head sea. In calmer waters, too, adjustment of the trim will help to optimise the boat's performance and/or fuel consumption by levelling it up if it is unevenly loaded with fuel or passengers. Remember, however, that by lowering the flaps you are, of course, increasing the boat's resistance to the water, so use only the minimum amount of flap, particularly at higher speeds.

The flaps can also be used individually to adjust the transverse trim of the boat. If you put the starboard flap down this tends to lift the starboard side so that the boat heels over to port. Put the other flap down and the reverse happens. Most modern motor cruisers of the medium to deep vee type run on an even keel most of the time but can be susceptible to heeling into the wind when there is a fresh wind on the beam. By lowering the windward flap in these situations the boat can be brought back onto an even keel. However, you should be aware that using the flaps in this way also affects the steering. Lowering the flap on one side of the boat increases the resistance on that side, tending to make the boat pull to that side. If you have the starboard flap lowered, you

A twin stern drive installation with power trim. Note the trim tabs at each side of the transom.

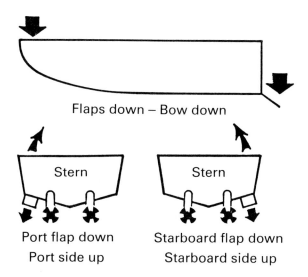

Flaps down – Bow down

Port flap down
Port side up

Starboard flap down
Starboard side up

TOP: *Putting both flaps down brings the bow down.*
BOTTOM: *Adjusting one flap controls the transverse trim of the boat.*

will find you have to put helm to port to compensate. Consequently you should use the minimum of flap to bring the boat up onto an even keel because this, coupled with the bias which you have to put onto the rudder, will serve to slow the boat down a little.

This steering effect described above can be put to good use as an emergency steering system. Simply lower the flap on the side into which you want the boat to turn and round it will go in a nice clean circle. If you then lift this flap the boat should stop turning. This is a fairly cumbersome method of steering, however, because the flap actuating mechanism tends to be fairly slow to react so that, instead of the steady course achieved with the steering wheel, you will tend to find yourself progressing in a series of wide sweeps. However, should your steering system and rudders fail totally the flaps can keep you heading in the right direction.

Flaps are only really effective above 12 knots or so, and would have little effect on displacement boats or planing boats below these speeds where the emergency steering facility becomes limited. Although it may get you home in an emergency, therefore, it will not be terribly useful for manoeuvring the boat right into your berth in harbour.

The flaps are usually controlled by dashboard mounted switches. Rather than actually indicating the way the flaps move, these switches are usually marked 'Bow Up' or 'Bow Down'. Alternatively the flaps may be controlled by a small joystick which is used in a logical way to control the trim of the boat both transversely and longitudinally. The biggest problem with flaps is knowing where they are at any time. Indicators have only recently become available, so the only foolproof way of checking the position of the flaps is to take them right up and start from scratch.

Propeller Trim
Propeller or power trim is found increasingly frequently on fast motor cruisers. It is a control system which causes a great deal of confusion, particularly amongst beginners. It is used on the more powerful outboard motors and stern drive systems, and consists of a hydraulic ram which moves the propulsion leg in or out from the transom. This has two effects. First, it alters the angle of thrust from the propeller in relation to the hull and second, it brings the propeller closer to the surface when the drive is trimmed out. Altering the line of the propeller's thrust in this way lifts the bow when the drive leg is trimmed out and drops the bow when the leg is trimmed right in. Bringing the propeller closer to the surface makes it operate in a semi-surface piercing form. This means that only the bottom blades which are running in a cleaner flow of water are doing the real work, and strangely enough the propeller becomes more efficient in this mode.

Power trim used in this way tends to be a feature of the higher performance motor cruisers and is used to obtain greater efficiency from the boat/drive combination. For example, it enables the boat to get quickly on the plane when heavily loaded. It is a feature that tends to be used for optimum efficiency when running boats at maximum power and when the longitudinal trim is fairly critical to obtaining the maximum speed. Hence, it can be used to good effect when operating a fast boat in waves, since the longitudinal trim can become critical in this situation. For most motor cruiser operations, however, the power trim is rarely critical and it is usually a case of trimming the drive leg out a certain amount for best efficiency. The amount can be determined in calm water by leaving the throttles set in a fixed position and then playing with the power trim control to get the maximum speed out of the boat. If you note the position of the trim control on the indicator dial you will be able to use this on future occasions when running the boat at speed.

One of the major stern drive manufacturers has introduced an automatic power trim control which trims out the drive leg when the engines reach a certain rpm. This saves you having to remember to trim out each time you open the throttles and trim in again when you slow down. This automatic trim system is quite effective for normal cruising operations although it lacks the subtlety of trim which is required for high performance racing boats.

When using power trim with the propeller close to the surface there is always the risk of cavitation (i.e. the propeller does not bite the water). You may notice this particularly when the boat is being turned at high speed. In this instance it is normal to trim the drive leg back in so that the propeller has a good bite on the water through the turn and then trim it out once the boat is on a straight course again.

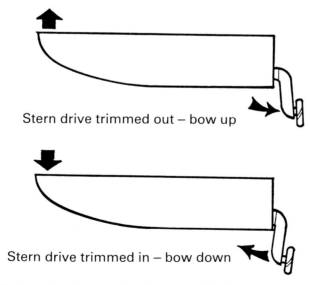

Stern drive trimmed out – bow up

Stern drive trimmed in – bow down

The effect on the longitudinal trim of the boat of trimming a stern drive leg.

The power trim is controlled by dashboard switches on a twin engine boat but with a single engine the switch is usually incorporated into the throttle lever so that you don't need to take your hand off the throttle to adjust the trim. However, coping with flap and trim controls as well as the throttle and wheel can be a bit of a handful and one sometimes feels the need for an extra pair of hands.

Throttles
After the steering, the throttles are the most important controls on the boat. Most modern motor cruisers have a single-lever control, where the throttle and gear change are incorporated in the same control box. With the lever upright the gearbox is in neutral and the engine is idling. Move the lever forward and you will feel it pass into a notch which indicates that ahead gear has been engaged. If you continue to move the lever forward the engine speed rises, and because the engine is now in gear the speed of the boat increases accordingly. The same thing happens as you move the lever backwards into reverse gear, although the throttle range in reverse is usually kept lower because you do not normally need full power when going astern.

Single-lever controls of this type give logical control when manoeuvring in harbour. For the inexperienced they are far preferable to having separate throttle and gear levers where good co-ordination is needed in order to achieve the right effect. There is always the temptation to open the throttle when the engine is not in gear or to try to engage a gear when the throttle is wide open. Either approach is not kind to the engine or transmission and the single-lever control makes this kind of mistake impossible. However, an analysis of boat handling in harbour shows that for most of the time only the gear is being engaged and the throttle is rarely opened beyond the idling point. This has led some fast boat designers to return to separate throttle and gear levers following the pattern used in offshore racing boats. Here the gear lever is used for harbour manoeuvring whilst in the open sea, the gears are left in the ahead position and the throttles are used to control speed.

One disadvantage of having the throttle and gear controls combined in a single lever is that the range of lever movement in the ahead position is somewhat limited. This tends to reduce the sensitivity of the throttle control. Whilst this is not a particular problem in most situations, when you are operating the boat in waves and trying to get the best performance out of it in these conditions this lack of sensitivity can make it difficult to match the speed to the conditions.

Opening and closing the throttle does not just increase or decrease the speed. Even on slow displacement cruisers the bow lifts when the throttles are opened and drops when they are closed. This effect can be used in some of the more subtle forms of boat handling, particularly if you get caught out in rough seas where you have to nurse the boat through the waves. In this situation opening the throttles can help the bow to ride over an oncoming wave and conversely closing the throttle drops the bow as the wave crest passes.

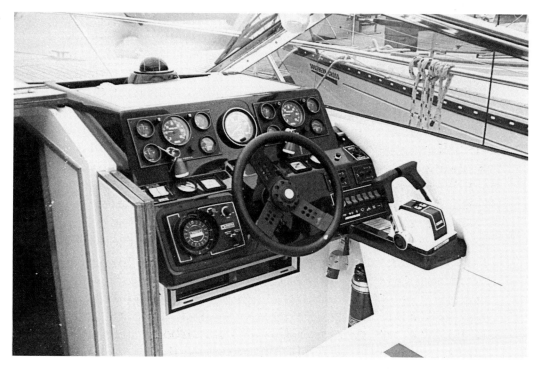

A crowded dashboard, which makes it difficult to get information or find switches in a hurry. However, the throttles and wheel are well placed for easy operation.

With single-lever controls, you need to be able to open the throttle without engaging gear when the engine is being started and warmed up. On some units this can be achieved by pulling out the lever sideways, which disengages the gear. Other control boxes have a separate lever which is used to set the throttle for starting.

TRIMMING THE BOAT

Before you become too confused, let me say that trim is not critical in a modern, well-designed motor cruiser. As a beginner you should concentrate on getting used to co-ordinating the steering and throttle controls. These are the two things that really count in boat handling. Trimming the boat is really a matter of fine tuning the performance once you have the boat running at a steady speed out at sea and the idea is simply to get the boat running on an even keel without the bow pointing to the sky or burying itself in the oncoming waves. It is in these situations that you start using the flaps and the power trim to keep the boat running at a comfortable angle, which can improve both the quality of the ride and the fuel efficiency. Adjusting the transverse trim with the flaps can make a great difference to comfort when you have a beam wind or at any time when the boat has a list because the waves will start to slam on the flat bottom of the hull instead of the deep vee hull giving a cushioned ride. You can also use the flaps to help cut down spray, which can cause visibility problems if the boat is leaning or if it is bow down.

In a displacement motor cruiser you have none of these controls; you simply have the steering wheel and throttles. Trimming the boat is largely a question of finding the right throttle setting for the sea conditions. It is possible to adjust the trim to a certain extent by moving weights around on the boat and for this you may be able to use a forward or aft fuel tank or even move people around on the boat, but by and large this sort of trim adjustment on a displacement boat is neither justified nor necessary.

You will note from this chapter that most of the controls are integrated in some way. The steering and the flaps affect each other, and the throttles and trim are related. In setting up the boat and getting it tuned to the sea conditions it is important to get the balance of the controls right. The boat should be running on an even keel, it should not be burying itself into approaching waves nor should it be pointing to the sky so that you cannot see the horizon ahead. The aim should be to find a good balance where the boat is running smoothly and comfortably. In the same way that you practised with the wheel and throttles in the early stages, now is the time to become familiar with the other controls. Practise first in calm conditions at different speeds and then graduate to waves, all the time watching the effect on the boat as you use the controls. This will give you the confidence to use them as they were designed.

3 · Boat Handling in Harbour

Manoeuvring a motor cruiser in the confines of a harbour is one of the trickier aspects of boat handling. However, providing you examine the position you are trying to get your boat into or out of, weigh up all the factors such as wind, tide etc which might influence the way your boat behaves once it is underway, and then work out how you can use the controls to counter these effects you will be far more likely to make a good job of it, even in difficult conditions.

Probably the greatest skill in boat handling is in weighing up the factors which might affect your boat, so we'll now take a look at some of these.

TIDES

The tide is a fairly straightforward factor to assess. It usually runs straight up or down a channel in a predictable way, although you may find strange eddies and countercurrents if there are solid jetties sticking out into the stream. In many marinas the tide may be very weak or non-existent, whilst in others there can be a strong flow. Before you set off work out the strength of the current and direction of the tide by looking at the flow past a fixed object such as a buoy or a post. If possible aim to be heading bow into the tide or current when manoeuvring at close quarters; this will give you a great deal more control over the boat. Heading into the tide, you can stop the boat in relation to fixed objects yet still retain steering control because the boat is moving through the water.

WIND

Wind is a much more difficult factor to cope with because it tends to be more variable, making its effect on the boat more difficult to determine. With most modern motor cruisers you will find that the wind tends to blow the bow away because the underwater section has less 'bite' on the water. Therefore if you have the wind on the beam the bow will tend to blow off down wind and this effect will be magnified at slower speeds. With the wind right ahead you will find that the bow will blow off in one direction or another and be harder to bring back once it starts to swing. A wind from the stern is much less likely to have any effect on the heading of the boat, although at slower speeds the effects of the wind will be more noticeable, especially if you have a cockpit canopy or hood up. It is quite disconcerting how a sudden gust of wind can ruin your carefully thought-out plans for coming alongside. The best way to assess wind direction and strength is by looking at flags or smoke but watch out for local variations when you are close to buildings or harbour walls.

LEAVING A BERTH

Leaving a berth is one of the simplest manoeuvres because you have plenty of time to plan before you begin and because you are moving away from solid objects rather than approaching them. As in all boat handling operations it is planning that makes perfect, so stop and think about the tide and the wind conditions and their likely effect on the boat; then work out a plan of campaign.

Using the Tide or Current

If you are alongside a jetty facing into a tide or current then you can let the tide do the work of getting you away from it. Simply put the wheel over to the side away from the jetty and you will find that the boat starts to drift away as you let go the ropes. A little nudge ahead with the engine will help the process, but before you use the throttle put the wheel amidships so that the stern does not swing into the jetty when you use the engine. This nudge with the engines will give you enough steerage way to ease the boat away from the jetty and then you can manoeuvre as you wish.

If the stern is lying into the tide or current then you should reverse this process and come off stern first. Put the helm over away from the jetty, and then with just a nudge astern with the engines the boat will drift away from the jetty. Once clear, straighten the boat up (or turn it right round, depending on which way you want to go) and off you go. Use the engines very gently when moving away to prevent the bow swinging into the jetty as the stern comes off, because at slow speeds the boat tends to pivot around a point somewhere close to amidships. As a result, if one end comes out the other end swings in, and it is quite easy to dent the pulpit rails if you do not keep an eye on the bow.

Using Springs
In both these situations the process of getting the boat away from the jetty can be made easier by using what is called a spring. This is a rope which leads from one end of the boat to the

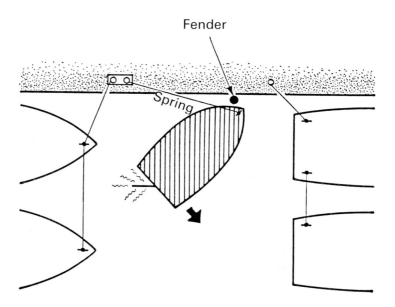

Using a spring to angle the boat away from the quay in a tight spot.

jetty adjacent to the other end of the boat. With the bow heading into the tide this spring would run from the stern of the boat and lead forward. When you let go every other line on the boat this spring holds the stern and lets the bow swing away from the jetty under the influence of the tide. You can reverse the process when the stern is into the tide and swing the stern off using a bow line lead astern. (Much the same effect can be achieved by giving a good shove off the jetty at the bow or stern, as appropriate, to start the boat moving.)

Using a spring is a useful technique to have up your sleeve if you find yourself in particularly difficult circumstances, perhaps when a strong wind is blowing the boat onto the jetty. In this situation, using the spring as described and going a touch astern on the engine will force the bow to swing off against the wind, hopefully enough to enable you to get away from the jetty cleanly, although you will need some smart rope handling and manoeuvring to get away before the boat is blown back against the jetty. The spring technique is also useful if you have boats moored close by ahead and astern.

LEAVING BOW FIRST

More and more often, motor cruisers tie up in marinas, which present a range of different circumstances when leaving your birth. Much will depend on whether you were brave enough to go stern first into your marina berth when you arrived, in which case leaving will be comparatively straightforward. You may be faced with a cross tide or wind, which pins you alongside the marina berth, in which case the only solution is to make sure you have fenders in place and then drive the boat out using engine power. You need to leave the berth fairly smartly in these conditions because once the bow is half out from the berth the wind or tide will catch it, the boat will pivot on the end of the marina pontoon and you may find the stern swinging out to touch your neighbour's boat. Smart use of the engines will ensure the boat leaves in a straight line. You can turn in the desired direction once the stern is clear. Always be ready to fend off from other boats.

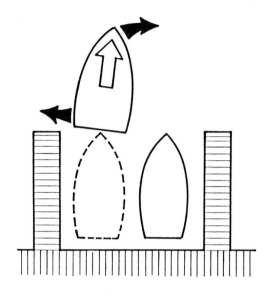

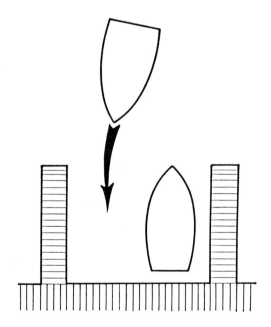

TOP: *Leaving a marine berth, don't turn the steering until the stern is clear of the pontoon.*
BOTTOM: *Entering the berth bow first is the simplest method.*

LEAVING STERN FIRST

Coming out stern first requires similar tactics. Try to keep the boat in a straight line until the bow is clear of the pontoon or adjacent boats before you start swinging. This can sometimes be more difficult because of the lack of steering control going astern and on a twin engine boat you are better off using the appropriate engine to keep the boat on a straight line. With stern drives or outboards you will always have much better control going astern because you are altering the line of the propeller thrust.

COMING ALONGSIDE

Before bringing your motor cruiser alongside, stop and work out exactly what you are going to do. Check the tide and wind conditions and relate these to the berth you plan to enter. Work out which side you are going alongside and attach fenders to the appropriate side. It sounds obvious, but do make sure the fenders are suitably adjusted for the height of the quay you are going alongside because in the final manoeuvring process your crew will not have time to adjust them as they will be busy handling the lines.

Using the Tide
If you are coming alongside a jetty with a tide or a current running parallel to it, the only sensible way to do so is head to tide. If you angle the boat at about 30 degrees across the tide to make your approach you will then balance the steering and the boat's speed against the way the tide is setting the boat in towards the jetty. As you approach the jetty bring the bow round to line the boat up with the tide. In this way, with a little practice, you should be able to hold the boat just a foot or two away from the jetty while the ropes are put ashore. It is very easy to hold the boat stationary simply by stemming the tide. Every so often give a touch ahead on the engines so that the boat is held level with a fixed point on the jetty. Then you can give the boat just a touch of helm in towards the jetty so that the tide sets it in slowly towards the berth; thus you maintain full control. Even if the gap you are

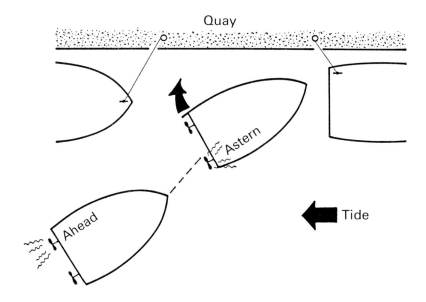

Coming alongside with a tide. A final touch astern should swing the stern into the quay tidily.

entering is little more than your boat's length it should not be too difficult to ease into it by delicate use of the throttle and steering wheel. In this way you can make good use of the tide to carry out manoeuvres which would be very difficult to achieve in its absence. The important thing to remember about this sort of manoeuvring is to use only a little helm and throttle and to make sure that the boat doesn't get too far out of line with the tide because it won't come back easily. The angle to the tide should never be more than about 20 degrees.

Without the Tide
To carry out the same manoeuvre with no tide running start in the same way by aiming the bow at about 30 degrees towards the jetty and steam in slowly, putting the engines into neutral as you approach the berth and letting the boat drift in for the final approach. At this point you can make subtle changes to the approach heading with the steering wheel or, with a stern drive or outboard, you will have to use the engines in conjunction with the wheel to maintain your course. When the bow is just a short

distance off the jetty a touch astern on the engine will halt the boat's progress. With a twin screw boat this touch astern on the engine furthest from the jetty will help to swing the stern in towards the jetty, so that you finish up comfortably alongside.

The temptation with this sort of manoeuvre is to stop the boat a little too far away. If you do this you can end up backing and filling with the boat in order to get one end alongside so that the crew can jump ashore with the lines. Keep the approach going right up until the last minute before you put a touch astern on the engines and in this way you will get the bow close enough to get a line ashore. Remember that the boat pivots somewhere near its centre point so that when you give the touch astern on the engine to bring the stern in the bow will swing off. Unless you have help on shore to tie up let the bow come in close so that the crew can jump ashore with lines.

BERTHING IN STRONG WINDS

Coming alongside is obviously complicated if there is a strong wind blowing. If the wind is blowing from the jetty out towards you, then you may need a steeper angle of approach to prevent the bow being blown off once you take the power off the engines. In this situation it may not be possible to get alongside quite so tidily, but the important point is to at least get a line ashore at the bow. You can always pull the stern in afterwards with the help of a second line.

When the wind is blowing onto the jetty, coming alongside can be a much more difficult exercise because there is very little you can do to prevent the boat being blown bodily onto the jetty. If there is a tide running you can use it as a cushion against the wind. Otherwise, the only real solution is to make sure you have good fenders out to absorb the impact. In addition, try to go alongside parallel to the jetty so that there are several fenders to absorb the shock.

MARINA BERTHING

This is another very tricky manoeuvre. First, there is often a distinct lack of space, giving you little room to manoeuvre.

Second, you often have to make a right-angled turn just before you enter the berth, which means that you cannot get a nice clean line of approach. And, of course, you will have to cope with wind and tide too. Once again, careful planning is the key to success, so that you will be able to anticipate problems, taking appropriate action before they occur.

The Approach

Making the initial approach down through the parallel lines of adjacent boats stay closer to the side away from your berth so that you have room to turn (remember your stern will swing out as you turn, so allow for this). But if you have any doubts, head straight down the middle. If there is a cross wind you will have to make allowances for this too (it will blow the boat bodily sideways since you will be travelling at slow speed).

At this point you should have decided whether you are going stern in or bow in to the berth; this decision will depend to a certain extent on the conditions. If there is a tide, current or wind running out from the berth, everything points to going into the berth bow first so that you have control over the boat right up until the last minute. If these conditions are reversed, berthing stern first may be more practical, particularly if your boat has twin screws. The real problems are likely to occur if there is wind against tide or if you have a strong beam wind, which can blow you sideways onto adjacent boats or hard onto the pontoon. As a general rule, if you have any doubts about the situation, it is safer to go in bow first because a boat is always more manoeuvrable when moving ahead than when moving astern.

Berthing Bow First

If you plan to go bow into the berth make your right-angle turn towards the berth just before you get to it (so that you approach the berth at a very slight angle). You want to keep steerage way on the boat for as long as possible, which with outboards or stern drives means keeping the power on right up until the last minute. A kick astern on the outboard engine should be enough to take the way off the boat as it enters the berth and will also help to swing the stern in to bring the boat parallel to the berth.

It is then simply a matter of running out the lines to hold the boat in position. The secret of this type of operation is not to make your right-angled turn too soon and to approach the berth at the correct angle, which is usually parallel or almost parallel to the pontoon. If there is a strong cross wind it pays to keep the power on as long as you possibly can to keep steerage way and to prevent the bow being blown off one way or the other. In any type of strong wind you need to get a line ashore as quickly as possible so that it can be used to control the bow once you lose steerage way.

Berthing Stern First

In general, stern first mooring in a marina is not usually necessary. It is much easier to go in bow first and then come out stern first, thus reducing the likelihood of mistakes, but if the tide or wind are setting into the berth then a stern first approach could be the right choice because you will have better control.

When coming in stern first take the boat past the berth, making allowance for the tide setting you towards the berth. Then give a touch astern on the outside engine, which should swing the stern round towards the berth. You may need a touch ahead on the other engine to complete the swing. Then it is simply a matter of backing into the berth using the appropriate engine to adjust the angle of the boat. The steering wheel will have no effect unless you have stern drives or outboards (and providing you have power at the propeller). Reversing in this manner requires a fair degree of skill and confidence. A more cautious approach would be to bring the boat up alongside the end of the finger pontoon, putting a line ashore and then either manouevring the boat into the berth by means of ropes or helping the process by using the engines. This would certainly be the right course to choose if you have a single screw motor cruiser which you want to berth stern first.

OUTBOARDS AND STERN DRIVES

Most of the above applies equally to all types of motor cruiser but it is worth pointing out the special features of handling a boat with stern drives or outboards. This can be very different to handling a boat with conventional propellers and rudders. The main point to remember is that as soon as you take the engines out of gear you lose steerage way to a large degree. The boat is then very quickly at the mercy of the wind and tide. It is a good idea, therefore, to keep the propellers turning as long as you can, which means you tend to come alongside a little faster than you would with other types of propulsion. If you do this in order to keep steerage way on the boat, you must be prepared to stop fairly rapidly and you often need more than just a gentle kick astern. Because you are actually steering by turning the propeller thrust, boats fitted with this type of propulsion tend to be much more sensitive. It also means that they have equally good steering power when going astern, which you can use to good advantage.

If you come into a berth at an angle you can take the bow almost up to the jetty, then turn the wheel towards the jetty and give a kick astern on the outboard engine. This will swing the stern in towards the jetty and bring the boat parallel to it. You do have to remember to use the wheel in conjunction with the throttles to successfully execute this manoeuvre. One often sees boats coming alongside where the skipper has forgotten to turn the wheel, so that when he tries to stop the boat the stern can swing out rather than swing in, to everybody's embarrassment.

Because of the very significant effect of the position of the wheel when manoeuvring boats of this type, a steering indicator is a very useful fitting to show the angle of the drive legs (propellers). You should turn the wheel before you put the engine into gear, either ahead or astern, so that the propeller thrust acts in the right direction.

Stern drives and outboards tend to be used in quite lightweight planing boats and there is often a fair amount of power available so that the thrust from putting the engines in gear can be quite vicious at times (hence the importance of making sure it acts in the right direction). It is usually best to manoeuvre these boats with a series of little nudges on the engine, putting it into gear for just a second or two. This will usually be more than adequate to get the boat moving in the desired direction. A slight steering effect is obtained from the leg of the outboard or stern drive unit when the propeller is in neutral but this is fairly minimal and is not enough to control the boat.

One advantage of having outboards and stern drives is the excellent manoeuvrability they give if you have to turn the boat round in a confined space. A series of bursts ahead and astern with the helm swung over from one side to the other as appropriate can enable you to turn the boat round virtually within its own length, even with a single propeller.

With twin propellers you use the conventional method of one engine ahead and one astern (the engine on the inside of the turn being put in the astern position). This type of turning manoeuvre will be assisted if you put the wheel hard over in the direction you want to turn. The same can apply if you are using a conventional propulsion system and turning round in this way, although the rudder will have less effect because it is not in the wash of the propeller going ahead.

MEDITERRANEAN OR STERN-TO MOORING

This system of mooring boats in marinas, widely used in the Mediterranean and some other parts of the world where there is a small tidal range, involves rather specialised techniques. With Mediterranean mooring the boat lies stern-on to the quay with the bow held out to seaward by means of an anchor or previously laid mooring. These berths are generally a tight fit but the mooring operation is simplified to a degree because there is usually a complete absence of tides or currents. It is therefore really a matter of reversing into the slot using a bow line attached to the anchor or mooring to check the astern movement of the boat.

Mediterranean mooring is simplest with a mooring buoy at the bow. As you approach the berth this is picked up first, a line is made fast to the buoy, and the boat turned until the stern is pointing into the gap you wish to enter on the quay. The next step is to let out the bow line as the engines are used to reverse the boat into the slot, and steering the boat using the appropriate engine. If all goes well the boat should slide into the slot, although fenders on each side of the boat are highly recommended. If the boat gets out of line with the slot, simply hold on to the line forward. This usually has the effect of straightening the boat. Alternatively, you can give a gentle nudge ahead on the engines to take the boat out and start the operation again.

Backing a boat into a slot in this way takes a little practice because everything seems back to front. It is the sort of operation you'll want to practise out in the open sea before attempting the real thing. On some motor cruisers there may also be a problem with visibility astern from the steering position; you will then have to rely on a crew member to guide you.

If you have to use your own anchor instead of a mooring buoy for the bow line then a little more skill is required. It is important to drop the anchor exactly in line with the berth you want to occupy. If you drop the anchor to one side or another, not only will you get an uneven pull as you fall back from the anchor, but

Mediterranean mooring. The slack line at the stern is the tail end of the bow line, which is passed ashore when you leave.

your anchor is also likely to foul those of the boats in the adjacent berths. Once the anchor has been dropped, back the boat down into the slot in the same way as if you were using the mooring buoy and make your stern lines fast onto the quay.

There is a third system which is used in some harbours; here you have to back the boat into the slot without the benefit of any line out at the bow. This requires more skill because you are handling the boat using only the engines, but if you line up the boat properly in the first place it should not be too difficult just to give a little power astern to ease it into the slot. With this type of mooring the bow line is left on the quay by the previous boat on departure from the mooring. Once your boat is in the slot pick up this line and pass it along the boat, pull it tight and make it fast at the bow. You are then, in fact, in the same position as with the other berthing systems, although you have achieved it by a different method.

Letting Go
With this particular type of mooring arrangement you pass the line ashore before you leave the berth, then let go astern and drive the boat gently out of the slot. Watch out for the bow line catching in the propellers; don't use them until you are sure they are clear. If the berth has a mooring buoy or if you have to use your anchor, let go at the stern first and heave in on the buoy line or anchor until the boat is out clear of the berth. You can then either let go the line or haul the anchor right up, and go on your way.

As with all mooring operations using this type of berth, it is a bit daunting the first time, but once you have had a little practice it becomes quite straightforward. If you take your boat to the Mediterranean you may be able to find a stretch of empty quayside where you can practise this type of manoeuvre before you have to carry it out close to other, expensive, yachts.

MOORING LINES AND FENDERS

Tying up the boat is an important part of the mooring operation which you must get right if you want to sleep on board or leave the boat with peace of mind. You need a couple of lines about 100 feet (30 metres) long and a couple of shorter ones which should be approximately the length of the boat. The long lines are used mainly when there is a considerable rise and fall in the tide, so that you can put out a good scope of line and not have to continually adjust it as the tide rises and falls. If you are going to be mooring in areas where there is a small rise and fall of the tide you could get away with four shorter mooring lines, although it is always useful to have one longer line on board which you can use as a tow rope.

Assuming you are lying alongside, you need lines out leading away from the bow and stern and two springs. The springs lead from the stern forward on to the jetty and from the bow aft on to the jetty. They prevent the boat from moving forward or aft, whilst the bow and stern lines hold the boat alongside. If you are only alongside for an hour or so you can get away with just a bow and stern line but it is never a good idea to leave the boat for any longer with just two lines out. If one of the lines were to part then the boat would be very vulnerable; with four lines the boat is reasonably secure. If there are strong winds or tides doubling the bow and stern lines will give added security.

The size of the mooring lines should be such that they are easy to handle and can be made fast on the available cleats or mooring bitts. It is no good having a large diameter mooring rope if you cannot secure it properly to the boat. Although it is always desirable to have good size cleats or bitts, these are not always available in practice, and you should size the mooring lines to suit your mooring facilities. Where the line passes through a fairlead or over the side of the boat it will be liable to chafe if it is left there for any length of time. Some sort of chafing guard is therefore necessary. This could be a piece of plastic tubing put over the mooring line or, as a temporary measure, a piece of cloth wrapped around the line.

When the boat is in its permanent mooring, which may be at a marina, you may want to make up lines which are exactly the right length so that they can be simply dropped over bollards or cleats at either end. This is both a tidy and efficient way of mooring and you can leave the lines ashore when you go off to sea. However, you still need alternative mooring lines on board for cruising.

Fenders are essential on a motor cruiser to protect your topsides. The most practical fenders are the cylindrical plastic type, which can be hung in the vertical position with a single line or hung horizontally with a line at each end. The horizontal attitude will give better protection if you are moored alongside a jetty with vertical piles, but using the fenders vertically is a better bet in most marina moorings. On permanent moorings you may prefer to use large balloon-type fenders to give better protection but these are difficult to stow on board. Cylindrical fenders are therefore the best bet for good all round use; make sure they are 'fat' enough to cushion the boat well.

On most motor cruisers you have to tie the fenders to the rails or stanchions along the side of the boat or even to inboard hand holds. None of these arrangements is particularly good because quite a lot of strain can be put on a fender when coming alongside or leaving a berth. A better arrangement is to have small cleats fitted along the toe rail for easy fender attachment. If you are doing a lot of canal or river work where the fenders can get stained with oil, a canvas sheet hung down over the topsides can give a measure of protection. It is also useful to have a plank fitted with a line at each end which can be put outboard of the fenders. This helps to give better protection when mooring alongside pilings or vertical fendering in locks. If you use your boat a lot in locks or canals then you might like to consider fitting a more robust and permanent type of fender to the hull to save constantly having to handle fenders. But before you fit this consider what effect it might have when the boat is out at sea.

LOCKS AND BRIDGES

Locks and bridges are a feature of many ports and harbours and if you take your boat cruising on inland waterways or rivers you will probably have to put up with more than your fair share, since they are necessary features of waterway navigation. Locks allow boats to move from one water level to another, the changing water level made necessary by tidal differences or simply by the need for a waterway to rise to a higher level. If you have a sea-going boat then probably most of the locks you need to negotiate will be manned — so there will be someone to operate

the lock for you. However, in some places boat owners themselves have to do the hard work, and it is as well to understand
the principles.

If you are moving from a lower level to a higher level through a
lock the water levels have to be equalised. First, the bottom gates
are opened. Once you have moved into the lock the bottom gates
and paddles are closed and the paddles which admit water
through from the upper level are opened. At this point there can
be quite a surge of water in the lock chamber so you should have
good mooring lines out to cope with this. Be prepared to adjust
them on board as the boat rises in the chamber. Once the water
has risen to the upper level the top gates can be opened and out
you go on your way. Before leaving a lock all the paddles and
gates should be closed.

Coming down through a lock the system is exactly the reverse.
If you are unfortunate enough to find the lock chamber empty
when you arrive you will have to open the paddles on the top gate
in order to fill the chamber before you can open the gates and
take your boat in. Never open the paddles on both the top and
bottom gates at the same time because this will simply allow
water to flow through the lock from the higher level down to the
lower level and you won't get anywhere. There is also a good
chance that boats on the higher level will go aground as the
water level is reduced.

Lifting, swing or other types of opening bridge are a feature of
many waterways and unless you have a very low air draft (the
height of the boat above the water) you will have to ask for the
bridge to be opened before you can pass through. Again, if you
spend a good deal of time on waterways you ought to know your
air draft fairly precisely so that you can judge your clearance
underneath bridges from the information provided on the chart.
Most bridges which open in one way or another are manned
because the road or rail traffic crossing them also has to be
stopped. There is usually a prescribed whistle signal you should
use to indicate your requirements to the bridge operator.
However, modern radio communication links by VHF are
becoming more common. By means of this communication
system the bridge operator can indicate just when the bridge is

likely to be opened so that you can be ready to pass through as soon as it does so.

RIVER NAVIGATION

Many rivers are navigable for seagoing motor cruisers, providing an interesting and alternative cruising area. The techniques of river cruising are very different from those on the open sea, as the bylaws and customs tend to vary in different

River cruising on a small displacement motor cruiser. The rounded transom corners are less vulnerable than hard edges.

regions or from river to river. You should equip yourself with the necessary chart or book which gives all the relevant information. Most navigable rivers are well equipped with locks and weirs to control the flow of water but even so, in times of flood, conditions can change quite rapidly. Debris can be quite a hazard, ranging from plastic bags which can cover your water intake or the propeller, to tree trunks which can cause more severe damage. Because of the limited room for manoeuvre the hazards may be very different from those you encounter at sea, so you will need to have your wits about you. Always have mooring lines and fenders ready for easy use. It is also a sensible precaution to have your anchor cleared ready for dropping quickly.

In many cases navigating in rivers is simply a matter of following the rules of the road and keeping to the right-hand side of the channel, but remember that shallows exist in many rivers – even those which have locks and weirs. As a general rule the deeper water will be on the outside of a bend in a river, but on straighter stretches the channel may not be so easy to find and an echo sounder can be very useful. However, although an echo sounder will tell you that the water is becoming more shallow, it will not tell you in which direction to head to find deeper water.

You are unlikely to find too many problems with navigation in the more popular rivers, but in a dry season when the water levels may be low you may have to navigate with a degree of caution. There are speed limits on most rivers – you must navigate at a reasonable speed to reduce the wash generated by your boat. This applies in harbours as well as rivers – you will not make many friends amongst other boat owners or the river or harbour authorities if you kick up a wash.

SINGLE-HANDED MOORING

If you have a smallish motor cruiser, say up to 30 feet (9 metres) in length, there is no reason why you should not operate it single-handed. This can often give you the chance to go boating when it is not possible to find a crew. There is a lot of pleasure to be had in operating a boat single-handed, particularly if you have an auto pilot, but the critical points come when you are entering and leaving your berth. Here you have to perform several tasks at once, and if you are to be successful you must plan things very carefully.

Leaving your berth is not too difficult, but you have to be fairly smart in letting go the lines and then moving swiftly to the wheelhouse to operate the controls. Depending on the circumstances, it may be possible to substitute one single temporary mooring line amidships for all the other mooring lines. If you have this mooring line on a bight so that it can be let go from on board you can then virtually release the boat from the steering position and still be in full control of the situation. Alternatively, it is often possible to let go the lines at one end of the boat whilst it is still held in position by the remaining line, thereby simplifying the casting off process. Once clear of the mooring you will need to stop and stow all the ropes.

Coming back alongside requires a little more preparation. Once inside the harbour or before you reach the restricted waters you should stop and put out fenders and get the mooring lines ready. How you arrange the mooring lines will depend to a certain extent on the conditions under which you are tying up, but one way to speed up the handling of the lines once you are alongside is to make one end of the line fast forward, pass it through the fairlead and then lead it outside the rails with a quick release hitch close to the steering position. The aft line is managed similarly so that these two lines are within easy reach of the steering position. Then as you come alongside and switch from using the engines and rudder to the mooring lines they are readily available as you jump ashore. It is then quite a simple matter to take a quick turn of each line round a convenient bollard. From then on you can finish mooring up at your leisure.

There is a little more still involved in single-handed mooring because you have to get the boat alongside and in a secure position before you can leave the controls and jump ashore. It calls for careful planning and good timing but it is a very satisfying operation to carry out efficiently.

4 · Boat handling at sea

MATCHING THE SPEED TO THE CONDITIONS

In harbour your problems tend to be those of handling the boat in close proximity to other boats and harbour installations. Out at sea you will come up against a whole range of different conditions to those in harbour, and there are many new techniques to learn. It is wonderful to leave harbour for the freedom of the open sea, heading out for the blue horizon, but the first thing you notice out there is that the surface of the water is usually far from calm. You may be lucky and choose a calm day. If you do make the most of it because calm days are comparatively rare and in most situations you will have to cope with wind and waves. The effects of these will be felt most if you have a planing boat because as speed increases the effects of the waves tend to become magnified. The secret of motor cruiser handling at sea is to match the speed of the boat to the conditions.

The handling techniques for displacement and planing boats are quite different. Displacement boats have a top speed of about 8 knots but a planing boat is likely to achieve speeds in excess of 20 knots, so you will have much more scope to vary the speed. With both types of boat, however, it is essential to match the speed to the conditions.

With modern motor cruisers the weak link in the whole system tends to be the crew rather than the boat and its equipment. The boats are generally built to a very high standard and are capable of taking considerable punishment from the wind and the waves. It is likely that the crew will start to object to difficult conditions long before the boat. Do not ignore the protestations of your crew — rather, heed them as a warning signal and try to find some way of improving conditions. When life starts to become uncomfortable it generally means that you are pushing the boat too hard. After all, in most cases you go out to sea in your motor cruiser for pleasure, so having a comfortable ride should come somewhere near the top of your list of priorities.

Even in a displacement boat, speed can have a significant effect on comfort. It is all a question of the speed of encounter with the waves. Hence, when you are travelling into a head sea with the waves coming towards you, your period of encounter with the waves will be much quicker and therefore the speed at which you travel is likely to be a lot more critical. In a following sea you can maintain a higher speed because the waves are travelling in the same direction as the boat and the period of encounter is much slower. In a following sea, therefore, unless the seas are quite rough, full speed will probably be the order of the day. However, there are other factors to be considered with following seas as we shall see when we look at this in more detail later on.

In a planing boat the higher speeds obviously increase the speed of encounter with the waves quite considerably, but to a certain extent the hull of the boat is designed to take this into account, and so you do not always have to ease back as soon as you might think. The warning signs come from the motion of the boat; if this starts to get too lively for comfort it is time to ease back. If the boat starts to fly off the top of the waves you are probably pushing things too hard, although this can be exhilarating in the short term and most good quality motor cruisers are built to take this sort of treatment.

THE EFFECT OF WAVES

It is not only the speed of encounter with the waves that affects the performance of the boat, but also the shape of the waves. In some conditions (usually when the wind is against tide) the waves are quite short and steep. Conversely, when the wind is with the tide there may be a flattening out of the waves and the change when the tide turns can be quite dramatic, particularly where the tides are strong. In any area where strong tides run you should be aware of this change because a nice gentle sea can, within the space of an hour or two, change into very uncomfortable conditions with short steep seas.

When waves become short and steep the wave length (i.e. the distance between the waves) also reduces – this means that the period of encounter is also speeded up. From all this you can imagine that life can become quite uncomfortable on board. In this situation it may not always be easy to match the speed of the boat to the conditions because the boat may not recover from one wave before it meets the next. The best advice I can give you is to avoid short, steep seas if at all possible, but if you can't then attempting to match your speed to the conditions is particularly important.

When handling any motor cruiser at sea you need to have a reasonable understanding of waves because they have a very significant effect on the boat. Waves are generated by the wind

A popular US type of fast cruiser giving comfort at sea and in harbour.

acting on the surface of the water. In winds of up to about Force 3, the waves generated under normal conditions are not likely to have very much effect on the boat. It is only when the wind starts to freshen that the waves increase to such a size that you will have to adjust your speed to suit the conditions. Waves are very rarely regular, since the surface of the sea is made up of several wave trains which are crossing. The main waves come from the direction of the wind, but there are usually residual waves and swell from previous blows which tend to make the waves irregular and, to a certain extent, unpredictable.

If you consider the average wave height for any set of conditions, then every so often waves will come along which may be twice the average height, or even bigger. This accounts for the fact that every so often as you are going along at a nice steady speed you will suddenly encounter a bigger wave which catches you unawares and throws the boat about in a disconcerting fashion. These larger than average waves should serve as a warning. Ideally, the speed at which you travel should be well within the limits of a comfortable ride so that you have something in reserve when these large waves come along.

Another feature of waves is the way in which a wave crest can have high and low points. This is generally caused by the interaction of different wave patterns and can account for the uncomfortable ride which is often experienced in beam seas. You should also be aware of the effects on waves of the wash caused by passing ships. This is something you have to watch out for, particularly in a planing boat, because it can catch you unawares and you can suddenly find yourself faced with waves which are considerably larger than those you had been experiencing. Whenever you see a ship steaming along at speed (or even another large motor cruiser), you should be aware of the wash that will be created by it. This is the time to keep your eyes open for those bigger than normal waves that can make life so uncomfortable.

One final point to remember is that the shape of a wave is not even. The windward face of a wave always has a more gentle slope than the leeward face, which can be quite steep. This means that when you are going into a head sea you face the steep side of the wave but have a more gentle slope when you get over the crest. In a following sea you have a comparatively gentle ride up the back of the wave, but there can be quite a sudden steep drop on the other side. This steepness can be exaggerated quite considerably if the wind is against tide, and it is the steep leeward face of the wave that can cause most of the trouble. If this face becomes particularly steep and unstable, as can often happen in strong tides or in strong winds, the wave can break. Breaking waves produce a moving body of water that has considerable power, and in these sea conditions you will need to handle your boat with considerable care.

HANDLING IN HEAD SEAS

Planing Boats
Head seas produce the most uncomfortable ride for any motor cruiser because the period of encounter with the waves is more rapid. The period of encounter is a combination of the boat's speed and the speed of the waves, so you could reach a situation where the bow of the boat has not fully recovered from one wave before it has to lift to the next, so it gets out of step with the waves and starts to give you a rough ride. Simply easing back on the throttles can make the ride more comfortable. You should find a speed at which the boat rides the waves fairly comfortably. Once you have found this speed you can set the throttles and relax a little, but bear in mind that the larger than average waves can come along unexpectedly so your hand should never be too far from the throttles. In more moderate seas you can be more relaxed about the throttle setting – but remember the problems with unexpected wash we have already discussed.

It is possible to drive the boat through head seas to make better progress by matching the speed much more closely to the conditions. To do this you adjust the throttle speed to *each* wave, watching out for the big ones that might approach from ahead. Racing boats are driven in this way, and it can be quite exhilarating to drive a planing motor cruiser in much the same way. This type of driving requires considerable concentration, however, because you have to read every wave as it comes towards you and adjust the speed accordingly. In diesel-powered cruisers you might not always get the rapid response from the engines that you need in order to vary the speed quickly. The idea here is to keep the boat going as fast as the conditions will allow without flying the boat.

In a head sea the bow does tend to fly up into the air as it meets an oncoming wave, and if you drive too exuberantly the whole boat can fly out of the water with the momentum it develops as it lifts to the waves. With a deep vee hull the re-entry is cushioned to some extent but flying the boat puts fairly heavy stress on the hull, on the machinery, and of course on the crew, so it is not recommended except for short periods. Even then it is not an efficient way of driving the boat (though it may look spectacular) because as the boat leaves the water the propellers become ineffective.

It is in these conditions that some of the other controls on the boat, such as flaps and power trim, can be used to good effect. The stern drives or outboards should be trimmed in to give the propeller a better bite on the water. This helps to keep the bow down. Even more effective under these conditions is the use of flaps. By putting the flaps down you will notice a significant drop in the bow; this can help to delay the moment when it comes unstuck coming off the top of a wave. Adjust the flaps gradually, a little at a time, so that you can see the effect. If you suddenly pull the flaps right down you could find the bow immersing into the wave rather than lifting over it. As with most other aspects of motor cruising, a comfortable balance is what you are striving for when adjusting flaps and power trim.

When you are running in a head sea and you see a large wave approaching, the tendency is to pull back the throttles and reduce speed. We have already seen in Chapter 2 that if you pull back the throttles the bow drops, and the sudden change in speed could cause the bow to bury in the wave. Certainly, there is a need to ease the throttles so that you don't charge into a big wave at full speed, but the emphasis should be on the word 'ease' so that you drop the speed just a *little* and don't pull the throttles right back so that the boat comes off the plane. By doing this there will be little change of attitude, but you will be at a more comfortable and resilient speed to meet the bigger wave and ride over it without any problems.

Displacement Boats

Many of these comments apply equally to displacement motor cruisers running in a head sea, and, indeed, if you are in a planing motor cruiser and the conditions become uncomfortable to the point where you have to operate off the plane you should still adopt very similar tactics. Finding a comfortable speed is the secret of success – the boat should lift comfortably over the wave without too much fuss or bother. With a displacement boat or a planing boat off the plane there is always a greater chance of the bow burying in the wave because the bow is more deeply immersed in these

The way flaps which operate on the water flowing away from the transom can be seen on this sports fisherman.

circumstances anyway and doesn't have the same buoyancy as a boat up on the plane. Planing boats which are off the plane can be particularly susceptible to burying their noses, or at least scooping up the top of the wave over the bow, because the bow is usually fairly fine and not specifically designed to cope with these speeds. To avoid the problem ease off the speed a little more, but still maintain good steerage way otherwise you could find a big wave will knock you right off course. This is only likely to happen when you encounter stronger winds and more violent seas, and if this sort of situation arises it is probably time to head for home. However, these conditions can develop quite rapidly as with a change of tide, so if this is the case it would be advisable to head in some alternative direction rather than straight into the waves.

HANDLING IN BEAM SEAS

In a beam sea the techniques for handling planing and displacement boats are very similar. In beam seas rolling is the problem, rather than pitching. Depending on the boat, the rolling may not be too uncomfortable, and running in a beam sea can often be quite a comfortable way of making progress, at least until the sea starts to become rough. Displacement boats tend to be more affected by beam seas than planing boats because the latter have much greater stability when travelling at higher speeds due to the dynamic effect of the hull on the water surface. A displacement boat can roll quite uncomfortably in a beam sea and if the natural rolling period of the boat happens to synchronise with the waves, quite a dangerous situation can develop. There is a very simple remedy; alter course even just 5 or 10 degrees and you will probably find the motion of the boat changes dramatically. Therefore, in a beam sea, it is not usually a good idea to operate with the sea fully on the beam. Instead, alter course a few degrees, just to introduce a slight crossing element into the waves.

Apart from rolling, a beam sea can result in a fairly unpredictable motion, because at one moment you are running along the very uneven crest of a wave, and at the next making progress along its very uneven trough: the sheer unpredictability of the motion can be exhausting because it is so very difficult to anticipate. The part of the wave that usually causes the most trouble is the steeper leeward side because, with very little warning, you can often find yourself running on the crest of a wave and suddenly dropping down the steep face into the trough.

Operating in a beam sea is rarely dangerous unless the waves are breaking fairly heavily. This is only likely to happen in a tide race or in winds of Force 6 or above, both of which you should be able to anticipate and avoid, so that on most occasions beam seas should not hold any terrors, although you may well have to cope with some discomfort. The level of comfort on board will be a good indication of whether you ought to take steps to improve the situation; only experience can help you decide what is a reasonable level of comfort for the particular conditions.

There are no particular techniques for operating in a beam sea. You can watch the seas ahead and you may be able to drive the boat around the bigger waves. You have the option of turning away from the sea and running from it or heading up into the wind and driving round the windward side of the wave. This latter technique can only be developed as you gain experience; in most instances when you are cruising for pleasure you are unlikely to find yourself in the sort of conditions where this technique has to be employed. In beam seas, as in other conditions, it is really just a question of matching your speed to the conditions, and quite often an increase in speed might be just as effective as a decrease when trying to find a speed at which the boat is more in harmony with the waves. Certainly, you have more freedom to adjust the speed in a beam sea because the stresses on the hull and crew will generally be much less than in a head sea.

HANDLING IN A FOLLOWING SEA

Following seas have a terrible reputation amongst boating people for producing conditions in which problems occur. There certainly are risks when driving a motor cruiser in following seas – but there are always risks when the seas get rough. It is only when there is a particularly heavy following sea that you are likely to find yourself at any real risk. In reasonable conditions handling in a following sea is quite straightforward, and as with all other conditions, if you understand the techniques involved the boat will operate more comfortably and efficiently.

Displacement Boats

In a following sea the waves will be overtaking you and there is not a great deal you can do to influence where the boat is in relation to them. The bigger the waves the faster they travel, but under normal conditions the waves will probably be travelling at between 15 and 20 knots – almost twice your speed. Small waves will have little impact; it is only when they are big enough to start lifting the stern, so that the bow is pointing downwards as they go past you, that you will have to start driving the boat more carefully. The steering tends to become erratic because the bow is buried in the water and the stern is up in the air. The boat then tries to pivot about the bow, so that you have a sensation of over-steering. Initially, you will find that the steering has no effect but the boat could suddenly take off with a rush and may turn almost beam on before you have a chance to correct it. This is known as broaching and a serious broach can leave you dangerously exposed beam onto the waves. This means that in a following sea with moderate waves running you can find yourself working fairly hard at controlling the boat. This is one situation in which you don't want too many turns lock to lock on the steering, otherwise you find yourself winding the wheel round to little effect. Quick, responsive steering is a great help to keep the boat running straight.

When you find yourself working overtime on the steering, winding the wheel from side to side to try to keep the boat in a straight line it is time to find an alternative course, although unless the waves are breaking you are probably safe from all but a large, breaking wave which arrives unannounced. Varying the speed may also help to improve control over the steering but do not slow down too much or you may lose steerage way.

At what stage the steering on a motor cruiser becomes difficult depends a great deal on the type of boat you have. If you have a displacement boat with a fairly fine bow, or even a semi-displacement boat operating at slower speed, you may well find that the steering becomes difficult to control in comparatively moderate seas because the bow buries itself and acts as a fulcrum which the boat tries to spin around. A boat with a big full bow and cutaway forefoot will lift readily on the waves even though it is angled downhill and is far less likely to bury and thus act as a pivot. The size of rudder also has a bearing on the way the boat handles; a good sized rudder which has a powerful steering effect is better in this situation than a smaller, less effective one.

In a following sea (with a displacement boat) the solution is not to ease back on the throttles, but rather to open them further because you get better steering control the faster you go. However, the motion of the boat can become quite uncomfortable in these situations because of the sudden change in angle as the wave passes under the boat. You may find that the boat, when angled with the bow down, tends to rush forward because of the downhill slope and then virtually stops as the wave passes under the hull and the boat adopts a bow up position. If the motion becomes too uncomfortable you may have to resort to driving the boat on the throttles, opening them wide to drive the boat up the slope and then easing them a little as the boat comes over the top.

Planing Boats
A planing boat is much easier to handle in following seas than a displacement boat. On a planing boat you have the option of overtaking the waves rather than having them overtake you. This enables you to dictate where you are in relation to the waves. One of the most comfortable positions is to be gently overtaking the waves, so that if the waves are travelling at 20 knots you want to be travelling at around 25 knots. This will mean that you have enough power to climb up the back of the wave. There will be a sudden change in attitude as you go over the crest, when the boat runs downhill before it lifts once more to the wave in front. Because the boat is only overtaking the waves at a gentle speed, you should be in full control of the situation and the ride will be fairly comfortable except when the boat changes attitude as it overtakes the wave crest.

You have a certain latitude to vary the speed, perhaps to try to find a more comfortable ride. But in general you won't want to drop below the speed of the waves because the small rudder fitted to planing boats means that you may find yourself having difficulty maintaining steering control. The worst situation is to find yourself just matching the speed of the waves as the rudder can became virtually ineffective, leading to the possibility of a broach. With stern drive or outboard powered boats this would not apply and you have more flexibility both in control and in speed because you have positive steering at all speeds.

In a planing boat you can run before a following sea even when the seas are quite big and it can be a very exhilarating ride. Although you feel fully in control of the situation you may not always appreciate that conditions are deteriorating. If you find yourself in a freshening wind running before the sea it is a good idea not only to keep a lookout astern but also occasionally to stop, turn round and head into the sea to get a better indication of how the conditions are developing. It is very easy when running downhill to be lulled into a false sense of security only to find, when you are entering harbour or having to alter course, that you are faced with very unpleasant conditions which you hadn't fully appreciated. Turning round in this way will not change the conditions, but it will make you aware of the developing conditions early on so that you can take necessary precautions, such as running for shelter or looking for an adjacent harbour.

THE CREW AT SEA

Already in this chapter we have noted how, in general terms, you will aim to drive your boat to give the crew a comfortable ride. On a long coastal passage this can be quite important, since tiredness can have a detrimental effect on your reactions and can affect your decision making. Out at sea there will be no-one to help; a long passage in a boat moving about in the waves can leave you tired and in a vulnerable position should any form of emergency arise. Keep a careful watch on the stamina of your crew, particularly on a planing boat where the motion is often more violent than on a displacement craft and where you need to have your wits about you because things happen much faster.

The resilience of the crew may also be reduced on a planing boat because the motion of the boat can prevent you doing any cooking, including making hot drinks. So you may find yourself suffering not only from tiredness but also from lack of sustenance, which will combine to reduce your efficiency.

Seasickness is another aspect which has to be considered. It is very debilitating and even if only one member of the crew is suffering it can put extra strain on the rest. It is certainly something to be aware of and to take precautions against.

There are many proprietary cures for seasickness, the majority of which are tablets which must be taken before you go to sea. This presents a problem because you don't know you are going to be seasick until you get out there, by which time it may be too late to take the tablets because you can't keep them down. People are often reluctant to take the tablets beforehand because they can cause drowsiness. A new method of coping with seasickness is the use of small sticking plasters which are placed on the skin behind the ear. Chemicals are contained in them, and these are slowly absorbed through the skin. The advantage is that you can use this treatment even if you are feeling sick at the time. It certainly seems to be a major step forward in coping with seasickness, although in most countries these special plasters are only available with a doctor's prescription. They still cause drowsiness but if they cure the seasickness symptoms this can be a great morale booster, and is preferable to the incapacitation of seasickness.

BOAT HANDLING AT NIGHT

Darkness adds a whole new dimension to boat handling and puts a great deal more pressure on the crew. Firstly, you can't see any of the approaching waves very well, so to a certain extent you are driving the boat blind. Secondly, different navigation techniques are required at night and identifying shipping becomes a very different visual process. If the conditions are good, however, operating at night time can be a novel and rewarding experience, and it is not one to shy away from.

Ideally, your first experiences of night time cruising should be on somebody else's boat, with one experienced person in charge.

When you do go out in your own boat at night, do so when the conditions are good, with only slight seas, so that you will not be under any pressure from difficult sea conditions. This will allow you to concentrate on the other aspects of driving the boat at night, particularly concentrating on the identification of other shipping and shore lights. Making an overnight passage can be very satisfying but it requires a certain amount of planning and preparation.

The main problem in handling a boat at night in any sort of sea conditions is visibility. In many motor cruisers reflections on the inside of the windows will destroy your vision outside. In the same way, switching on lights in the wheelhouse or cabin areas can destroy your night vision. If you are going to be able to handle the boat properly in waves at night, you must be able to see properly. Perhaps the best solution is to use an outside steering position where your night vision will be much improved. You will find when you are outside that your other senses will also help your awareness of what the sea is doing and what the conditions are like.

A major handicap to night vision, even from an outside position, is the navigation lights which tend to cast their glow all over the forepart of the boat. It is very tempting to switch off the lights to gain better visibility but this is not particularly wise because there may well be another boat in your vicinity doing the same thing. Navigation lights are required by law, and before you venture out at night you should not only make sure that yours are working efficiently but also that you know and understand the lights used by the various types of boat and fishing vessel that you might meet. You can then take the appropriate action if they come near.

When driving the boat at night in waves use the same techniques as in daylight. Of course you will not be able to see the waves ahead, and the biggest danger will be from that larger than average wave which catches you when you are going too fast. At night time you will get very little warning of the approach of these waves, so you should cut your speed back even more than you would during the day, allowing a greater safety margin in your speed so that you have the scope to deal with unexpected conditions.

5 · *Leaving and entering harbour*

PREPARATIONS FOR GOING TO SEA

There is always a great temptation when you come down to your boat to simply start the engines, throw off the mooring lines and head out to sea. If you took the trouble to put your boat to bed properly when you last came into harbour you could probably get away with this but it makes a great deal of sense to get into the habit of always checking round the boat before you go to sea. This check should include the engines and the electronics but you should also check that everything is stowed away properly because once you are out at sea it becomes much more difficult to do any of these jobs. It pays to have a check list of the things you have to do, rather like the pilot of an aeroplane goes through certain checks before take-off. This list does not need to be anything like as comprehensive as an aircraft's but if you work through the following list to make sure that everything is operational then you will have the opportunity to sort out any problems in harbour, where you will have far better resources available to you.

The engines come near the top of the list; here it is mainly a matter of checking the oil and cooling water levels and looking for any leaks in the systems. Ensure that the necessary seacocks for the cooling system are open, and that seacocks on toilets and other domestic outlets are closed. Such a check is necessary for two reasons: you will be fully aware of the state of play with the seacocks at any time; and turning them frequently helps to keep them operating freely so that they will work properly in an emergency. Unfortunately in many boats the seacocks are not always as accessible as they should be. One of your winter jobs might be to improve this in some way.

Don't forget to check the fuel levels on the gauges and sight tubes, if fitted, and do a quick calculation to ensure you have an adequate reserve in case of bad weather or failure of an engine. If you are setting off on a reasonably long trip it is good policy to check the fuel filters and drain off any accumulated water. You may have a propeller shaft which has grease lubrication so a couple of turns on the greasing screw will keep the system running for a few hours before it needs attention again. Whilst you are doing this a quick glance at the stern gland will show whether there is any excessive water leaking through. If the gearboxes are fitted with dipsticks these should also be checked now, and turning the steering from hard over to hard over will ensure that everything is free and easy. Whilst you are in the engine compartment a quick look around to make sure that nothing is loose that might move around when the boat is out at sea is a wise precaution; then you can move up into the accommodation to look at the stowages there.

Stowing everything away before you go to sea should be one of your priorities. There is nothing more irritating than having equipment or gear coming loose when you are out at sea and having to stop to stow it. If your boat is well organised it should not take long to put everything away securely. The galley area is probably one of the most difficult places to secure things but time spent doing this thoroughly will be time well spent. After all, you will be avoiding the mess caused by breakage which can result if anything comes adrift. Check each of the lockers to make sure there is nothing which will rattle around, and then make sure that all the locker doors and internal doors in the accommodation are either secured open or closed as appropriate. If there is anything rattling around down below it can cause irritation and distraction when you are sea and could also cause damage because of the constant motion of the boat. Make a mental note of anything that comes adrift when you are at sea so that you can improve the stowage or security of that particular item when you are next in harbour. It is very easy to forget these irritations when you get back into harbour only to have them recur when you go to sea next time.

If you are going to sea for any length of time food and drink ought to be considered in advance. In a displacement boat there may be some possibility of cooking (or even just boiling a kettle) if the motion is not too severe, but on a planing boat these operations are generally out of the question unless conditions are very good. Sandwiches are the obvious answer as far as food is concerned and these should be made up before you go. Cold drinks can provide liquid refreshment but hot drinks are often much more welcome out at sea, so making up vacuum flasks of hot drinks is a good idea.

Clothing is another important consideration. It is very difficult to change clothing once you are at sea, except perhaps to put waterproofs on if you have to go outside. Remembering that it is usually cooler at sea than it is in harbour, common sense dictates that you don warm clothing before you go to sea; it is always easier to take off a sweater if the weather proves too warm. Feeling cold out at sea is very debilitating, so it is important to keep warm – both for your wellbeing and your pleasure. Warm clothing is particularly important if your boat has an open steering position where you will be exposed to the elements. If you are driving in the open air for some time, wear a hat to keep your head warm. It is not always easy to anticipate just what the conditions are going to be out at sea so, as far as clothing is concerned, be prepared for the worst.

Finally – navigation. If you plan your route on the chart before you go, laying off the courses and distances, life will be much easier when you are at sea. Chart work at sea can be very difficult, even if your cruiser is fitted with adequate facilities to lay out a chart. We will look at this aspect in more detail in Chapter 7.

You should also look up the relevant tide tables before you set out. If you use electronics for navigation then have these programmed with the waypoints you want to follow so that you have all the available information at your fingertips. This approach should take some of the panic out of navigating and you can set off knowing where you want to go and how you are going to get there. Also check the state of access at any intermediate ports you may have to make for in an emergency.

HEADING OUT TO SEA

A VHF radio is now almost essential on any motor cruiser and when you are leaving harbour it can be used to let the coastguard or the harbour authority know where you are going. You might argue that it is none of their business, but think of it as a safety precaution. If somebody on shore knows where you are heading, if you do not turn up because you are in serious trouble the rescue authorities will have some idea of where to start looking for you. But remember to follow the responsibility through and let them know when you have arrived, otherwise they may send out a search party. Remember also to let them know about any change in your destination. It can be very reassuring to know that somebody knows roughly where you are if you do get into trouble. Radio communication is a wonderful invention to improve safety at sea. As a motor cruiser owner you should take full advantage of the benefits it offers. Even if your boat is not fitted with a radio you can still let somebody on shore know where you are going by telephoning the coastguard or letting the marina staff know, but again make sure that you report in the same way when you arrive.

In some ports and harbours in Europe you are required to contact the harbour authorities before you leave your berth so that they have a list of boats that are moving about in the harbour. In most cases, however, the harbour authorities are not too concerned about your movements, provided you keep out of the way of shipping. A radio link with the harbour authorities can be very useful in those ports where there is traffic control. This is often the case in busy harbours with a narrow entrance, where you have to obtain permission before entering or leaving. The purpose of this is to avoid the risk of collision in these narrow waters; it will often be the case that you have to wait whilst a ship comes into the harbour. Although radio communications are used for traffic control, there are usually visual signals which can be found in the relevant pilot book for boats not fitted with radios.

Something else to watch out for in harbour is the speed limit. There are a growing number of harbours where a speed limit is enforced to avoid nuisance to other users – break these regulations at your peril! Speed limits are common sense in most cases and are usually confined to the restricted areas of the harbour. Details of speed limits will be given in the pilot book. Once you are out into more open waters nobody will worry about your speed.

There are three main types of harbour, each of which presents different conditions when you are leaving. The first of these is built with stone breakwaters, where you enter the open sea as soon as you pass through the entrance. This means that there will be a sudden transition from the calm of harbour to the open sea and you should be prepared for this. You may be faced with a quite lively motion on the boat once you have gone beyond the piers. (It is in this sort of situation that you will be thankful you have stowed everything away carefully beforehand.)

The second type of harbour is formed around a narrow river entrance, which is usually enclosed with piers to control the water flow and reduce silting. Here, too, there will usually be a fairly sudden transition from the calm of harbour to the lively waters of the open sea. In addition, because of the tides and currents, which can sweep in and out, you will often find nasty sea conditions in the entrance, particularly when there is an ebb tide and an onshore wind (which produces a wind against tide situation). This type of harbour entrance also often has shallow water either just inside or just outside the piers, and this 'bar' can make the breaking sea conditions worse. Sea conditions in this type of entrance are usually only bad when there is an onshore wind; on leaving harbour you will be going into the breaking seas, which is the best way to tackle them. If you have any doubts about leaving a harbour of this type it is a good idea to consult the locals. With a strong ebb tide you can often find yourself being swept into breaking seas before you realise it, so check out the expected sea conditions first.

The third type of harbour has a long estuary. Here the transition from harbour to sea is much more gradual and whilst this might make life easier in terms of adapting to the changing conditions, you will often have to cope with long and tortuous channels through sand or mud banks on the way out to sea. Here the challenge is one of navigation in waters where the channels are marked by buoys. You should follow the route from buoy to buoy but it pays to do a certain amount of preparation so that you know the courses between buoys. Then, if you cannot immediately pick out the next buoy, at least you know in which direction it lies. This preparation will also stand you in good stead if visibility deteriorates.

In general, heading out to sea is a fairly straightforward operation from most ports and harbours. At night, however, particularly once you have left the friendly lights of harbour behind and enter what appears to be a black void in which you have to pick up the distant winking lights of buoys to navigate, things can become much more difficult. At night, therefore, preparation is absolutely essential so that you know which courses to follow once you have left the confines of the harbour. It is an advantage to leave harbour when the tide is flooding because then, if you are not happy with the situation, you can always ease the speed and just stem the tide whilst you work things out. By doing this you still have the steerage way and control over the boat whilst making very little headway through the water.

APPROACHING HARBOUR

Approaching harbour, particularly if the harbour is strange to you, puts pressure on your navigation skills as well as introducing an unknown factor. But it need not be daunting – approaching a strange harbour can be an exciting and rewarding experience. As ever, planning is the key to success in this situation. Before you set out you should have studied the approaches to your destination harbour in order to try to build up a mental picture of what you might see as you approach. This mental picture may not be particularly accurate, but what you are really trying to identify are conspicuous headlands, lighthouses or other features which will help you to decide your approach. Once you have managed to work out where you are in relation to the harbour it is quite a simple matter to set a course in the right direction to pick up the first or fairway buoy of the approach channel. This is where the pressure starts to mount because you will be running into shallow water and other potential dangers. The buoys and other features in approach channels are usually placed there to help big ships rather than motor cruisers, and you will spend much of your time anxiously looking ahead to pick up the next mark or identify the leading marks which keep you in the channels so that you can make a safe approach.

Navigating during your approach to port is something that you can, to a certain extent, plan in considerable detail before you set out. Even if you cannot visualise how the approach will look you will have the chart in front of you and with the plotted courses and distances it should not be too difficult to work out your position. However, the weather conditions are not so easy to forecast and even more difficult to plan for, since they can mean that it is not safe to enter port. The weather conditions may be the critical feature of a port approach, particularly for smaller ports.

HARBOUR ENTRANCE CONDITIONS

The first thing you need to establish is whether there will be an adequate depth of water to make your entry. Many small ports rely on the rise of the tide to give adequate water for boats to enter and leave. So the first thing to work out on your port approach is what the tide is doing (ebbing or flooding) and whether the existing tide will provide an adequate depth of water for your approach. At the same time you need to work out the direction of the tide or current because this can have considerable bearing on the conditions in the entrance.

If we go back to the three different types of harbour described earlier we can look at the conditions you might find in each when making an approach. First, the harbour with stone jetties running out to sea. This type of harbour usually has a reasonably clear deep water approach and even if it is a tidal harbour (Europe) the entrance is usually fairly straightforward. However, if there is an onshore wind waves running up against the piers may be reflected back and this can sometimes create a confused sea just off the harbour entrance. It can be quite disconcerting to encounter these conditions just when you think you are almost safe in harbour. In a strong wind a very nasty sea can be generated by these reflected waves but this is usually only the case when there is reasonably deep water right up to the piers and when the piers themselves have vertical outside walls. Many modern breakwaters have sloping or broken seaward faces which do not reflect the waves in the same way, thus reducing the risk of broken water off the entrance.

The second type of harbour with a narrow river entrance protected by piers is probably the most dangerous and needs to be approached with considerable caution, particularly when there is an onshore wind. This type of harbour is often associated with a bar which may have shallow water over it. With an onshore wind and an ebb tide flowing over the bar there will be a potentially dangerous breaking sea in the harbour entrance. This breaking sea will generally be in the region where the water is shallowest and may occur outside the actual entrance piers or just inside them depending on the harbour, the state of the tide and the wind.

The main problem is that it is very difficult to judge the sea conditions in the entrance when viewing them from seaward. This means that you could be making your approach in comparatively good conditions, and certainly ones which do not give you any cause for concern. The harbour entrance may not look particularly alarming either, because you are viewing it from the windward side and the waves will be breaking down to leeward so that you will not see the full impact. Contact the harbour authorities by radio to ask their opinion if you are doubtful, particularly if there is an ebb tide. If radio contact is impossible it would make sense to wait for slack water or for the flood tide before making any attempt to enter. On the flood tide, wind and sea will be in the same direction, making for calmer conditions. If you have a displacement motor cruiser and you find yourself in amongst breaking waves, battling against strong ebb tide, you could be at risk of broaching to, i.e. turning beam on to the waves with very little room to manoeuvre within the confines of the piers.

In a planing boat you have a better chance of coping with these conditions because your greater speed means you can sit on the back of a wave as you drive into the harbour and only overtake it once it has broken in front of you. This sort of manoeuvre requires a fairly strong nerve and considerable experience because once you are committed there is no turning back. In larger harbours of this type which have deeper water there is less risk of the sea breaking in the entrance unless there is a strong wind blowing outside.

In the third type of harbour, where the entrance is up a long estuary, you should find increasingly better conditions as you move further up the estuary. This type of entrance may place greater demands on your navigation capabilities than on the seaworthiness of the boat. In estuaries you may find small areas of breaking water, particularly when there is wind against tide in narrow channels where the tide can be particularly strong. In general this type of harbour should not pose any problems except perhaps from the point of view of the navigation skills needed to find the off-lying buoy or lightship marking the beginning of the entrance. Because there may be no land features in the vicinity you will need to navigate with accuracy, particularly when the visibility is not good, in order to find a landfall mark.

Under the majority of conditions in which you will normally be cruising harbour entrances should not pose any undue problems and the risks involved in entering harbours may only become apparent when you are seeking shelter from a freshening wind and conditions are deteriorating. This will be true particularly if you have been running downwind to look for shelter because it is in these circumstances that you will find harbours facing an onshore wind where the conditions could be difficult.

ENTERING HARBOUR

It can often be a strange feeling approaching a harbour entrance because although you have the chart spread out in front of you it may bear very little relation to what you actually see. The features which appear to stand out clearly on the chart, such as piers or jetties, all appear very flat and undistinguished against the land and the entrance to a harbour can be quite difficult to pick out until you are fairly close. Ideally you want to pick out a distinct feature from the chart such as a church spire, a water tower or lighthouse which stands out clearly and which will give you a good guiding direction to steer towards to find the harbour entrance. When you are a mile or two off, the entrance should become clear and you can then approach with more confidence.

If you have a radar on board the picture will be much clearer because the radar picture can be matched to the picture shown on the chart. Also it is often easier to pick out piers and entrances on the radar screen than to pick them out with the naked eye. Remember, though, that the radar beam is only 'viewing' the harbour from much the same angle as you, so that, in theory, it will not see a great deal more than you can. However, the radar has the advantage of being able to measure distances, so that it can distinguish landmarks much more precisely from the land behind. Radar can thus be a great asset when entering harbour, particularly at night.

Making a harbour approach at night can be one of the most difficult situations and here it is always better to stop and work out where you are and what is happening rather than carry on blindly in the hope that things will become clearer as you get close.

Approaching a UK or European harbour, it is always wise to make contact with harbour authorities on the radio if they have a harbour link so that you can announce your entrance. This is usually just a quick call to obtain approval for entering but often you will also get information about shipping movements taking place inside the harbour. When inside the harbour you will suddenly be faced with other craft as well as jetties and piers and you may need to have your wits about you. If you have done your planning beforehand you will have worked out roughly where you want to go. If the harbour is strange to you the logical place to stop and catch your breath is in a visitor's berth, now a feature of many harbours and marinas.

In theory, visitors' berths are an excellent idea because they give you somewhere to head for immediately. You can obtain information about a more permanent berth or even stop there for a short time. Visitors' berths can become very crowded, however, and it is not unusual to find yourself approaching a berth only to find that there is no space left or that you are left with the option of going alongside one of the other boats already in the berth. Faced with this situation you can, of course, go into any berth which is vacant provided you are only doing so on a temporary basis just to sort yourself out; there could well be an owner with his boat not far off who wants to enter his rightful slot.

Harbour and marina staff are usually helpful (after all, you will be paying for the berth). Problems sometimes arise at very busy times of the year so it is often a good idea to phone ahead and try to book a berth or a mooring rather than just arriving on spec. There is nothing worse than arriving in harbour after a long passage only to find there is nowhere to tie up for the night.

HARBOUR FORMALITIES (UK and Europe)

Virtually every harbour, whether it is a marina or a commercial harbour, has its paperwork and if you want a quiet life it pays to conform. In most cases this will simply be a question of paying your fee for tying up for the night and obtaining a receipt, but if you have arrived from a foreign country the formalities are more strict.

First, you should fly the yellow Q flag to signify that you have arrived from abroad; before you allow any of the crew to wander off you should get Customs clearance. Sometimes Customs officers will come on board, or you may have to go to their office. The marina or harbour staff will generally advise you; it pays to co-operate as Customs can make life difficult for you if they want to. In some cases you may also need health clearance and the immigration authorities may wish to check your passports, etc.

The most important piece of paper which all these authorities will want to see is the vessel's documentation. Rather than keeping the original on board it is usual to keep a series of copies which can then be handed out to the various authorities as required. To become a documented vessel the boat has to go through a Coast Guard inspection.

If you are planning to visit a foreign country you should do some research about the entry formalities for that country. Requirements vary, but generally you will need the yacht's documentation, copies of the crew list, passports and clearance from Customs at the last port you visited. Be prepared for a certain amount of form filling, take the formalities seriously and you should have no problems. Before you leave your home port clear your departure with Customs and possibly the immigration authorities so that everyone knows your plans. Leaving harbour for home waters requires no formalities other than letting your proposed passage plans be known to the coastguard or other authority. You don't have to stick rigidly to these plans, but if you do change your mind call up on the radio to let these people know. Most importantly, inform them you have arrived safely in port or they might initiate a search for you.

6 · Anchoring and mooring

Anchoring is a great act of faith. If you stop to consider what you are doing (throwing a lump of metal over the side on the end of a piece of rope or chain and expecting it to hold your boat securely) you can see where the faith comes in. This faith can be justified because hundreds of years of development of anchors ensures that they dig firmly into the sea bed and provide the means to hold the boat secure. However, since you cannot see the anchor on the sea bed or what is happening to it you need to understand something about anchoring techniques.

Often you will use your anchor as a means of escape from the crowds. For many boat owners, the joy of ownership comes from escaping to the freedom of the open sea. There is a limit to how much time you want to spend underway motoring around, however, and the dream of finding a quiet spot to drop your anchor can be one of the attractions of boating. Such isolated areas may be hard to find in today's crowded cruising waters, but using an anchor can certainly extend the use of your craft and in this way the boat can make a fine bathing platform or can be used as a picnic base close to a picturesque coastline.

There is also a more serious side to anchoring – that is for use in emergencies. In a single-engined boat the risk of engine failure and consequent disablement can be an ever-present concern. If this happens, the chances are you will find somebody to tow you back, but the anchor provides a long-stop protection if you find yourself drifting ashore with no help in sight. In these circumstances you will certainly need an anchor that is going to hold firmly in a variety of different bottom conditions. Even with a twin-engine boat the risk of engine failure or getting a rope around your props still exists, so the anchor is an important part of your safety equipment.

ANCHORS AND LINES

There are a wide variety of anchors to choose from on the market today, ranging from the traditional fisherman's anchor right through to the modern Bruce anchor. Each of these different types has advantages and disadvantages, but one of the most important considerations is the stowage of the anchor. Anchors such as the Bruce, Danforth and the CQR can be stowed snugly at the bow where they are ready for instant use. The Bruce anchor probably has an advantage over the others because it has no moving parts which can wear or corrode, but it can be awkward to stow flat.

Whilst stowage is important both from the point of view of appearance and practicality, the overriding consideration in selecting an anchor should be its holding power on the sea bed. Holding power is related to the design of the anchor, its weight and the type of line or chain. For holding power under a wide variety of different sea bed conditions ranging from rocks to soft mud the traditional fisherman's anchor is probably the most versatile – it is certainly one of the few which has a good chance of holding on a rocky bottom. However, it is less efficient on softer bottoms such as mud and sand, and here the CQR and the Danforth anchors offer greater efficiency. The Bruce anchor and various equivalent modern designs following the same concept are equally good in this respect, and combined with the self-stowing characteristics of these anchors they tend to be a favourite amongst motor cruiser owners.

Anchor Weights and Line Lengths
The weight of the anchor must be matched to the size and type of boat it has to hold. As a general rule, the weight of the anchor in pounds should be the same as the length of the boat in feet, although lightweight planing boats could probably get away with a 20% lighter anchor. You should bear in mind, however, that if there is high superstructure its windage can add to the strain on the anchor, so don't be tempted to cut corners too

much. Conversely with heavy displacement boats, a 30 footer (9 metres) could weigh twice as much as a light planing boat of the same length and will therefore need a heavier anchor.

There is always a tendency to go for the lighter anchor, particularly on planing boats where the extra weight and the problem of stowing a heavy anchor securely can be a disadvantage. You also have to consider how easy it is to handle the anchor, particularly when there is no power assistance on board. A lightweight anchor will do the job quite happily in many circumstances, for example when you wish to anchor in fine weather for pleasure purposes, but when deciding on the weight of anchor to carry always bear in mind the emergency role of the anchor.

Another factor which can have a bearing on the size of anchor is the line or chain attached to it. It is always best to have all chain because the weight of the chain can be a major contributory factor in getting the anchor to hold securely. Much of the chain will lie along the sea bed so that the pull on the anchor itself comes in a horizontal direction; this gives it a better chance to dig into the sea bed and hold properly. For the same reason the more line you put out on the anchor the better it is likely to hold because this reduces the high strain on the line when the chain jerks tight. On a 35-foot (11 metre) motor cruiser you will need 200 feet (60 metres) of anchor chain, with an extra 10 feet (3 metres) for every 1 foot (⅓ metre) of extra length on

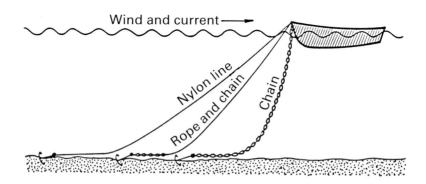

How the weight of the anchor line varies the way in which the line will lie. Chain is best because there is more spring in the line but a combination of chain and rope is a good compromise.

larger boats and a similar reduction down to a minimum of 100 feet on smaller cruisers.

Now 200 feet (60 metres) of chain can weigh quite a lot, which may not be acceptable on a fast planing motor cruiser. Most therefore end up with a compromise anchor line which is part chain and part rope. If you adopt this combination the first 20 or 30 feet (6–9 metres) of the line should be chain to give added weight to the anchor to help produce the horizontal pull on the anchor itself and to reduce chafe on the bottom.

Windlasses

On motor cruisers of 30 feet (9 metres) and upwards it is becoming increasingly common to find an anchor windlass fitted to help handle the anchor. These come in a variety of shapes and forms and they can be hand or electrically powered. Electric power takes the hard work out of recovering the anchor and also enables the recovery operation to be carried out from the wheelhouse or flybridge by remote control. The whole anchoring operation can thus be a single-handed job.

There are two main types of anchor windlass, one with a horizontal shaft and the other with a vertical shaft, the latter increasing in popularity. Here the chain is led from the bow roller around the windlass and then forward again before it drops down the spurling pipe into the chain locker. With the horizontal type the chain leads over the windlass and the spurling pipe is placed immediately below so that the chain drops down into it. Either type is equally good and both can have a small capstan fitted on top, so that it can still be used if you have a combined rope and chain anchor line. However, with this type of line you cannot have an automatic system controllable from the wheelhouse. The general trend is to have an anchor line which is all chain if you have a windlass because this simplifies the recovery operation.

Anchor Stowage

The anchor is stowed in a fitting which is mounted at the stem. There are a variety of patented fittings on the market; they usually consist of one or more rollers, and when recovering the anchor the shank is automatically pulled into the rollers and secured by the tension of the anchor chain. This is a tidy arrangement but there is also a need for some additional securing device, perhaps in the form of a pin. The anchor must be tight enough to prevent *all* movement, particularly in lively sea conditions where the bow might bury into a wave and put considerable stress on the anchor and its stowage. On smaller boats the anchor may well be stowed inboard and because of its weight and potential to cause considerable damage if it becomes loose it should also be stowed securely. Many craft now have a small bow locker for stowing the anchor and its line; but you must make sure that it is well secured and not loose in the locker.

Two useful points to remember when stowing the anchor and line are first, make sure that all shackles are securely moused, and second, that the end of the line is made fast in the chain locker. Mousing shackles prevents them becoming unscrewed when they are on the sea bed, which could allow the anchor and line to separate. Mousing is carried out by passing a piece of wire through the shackle pin and around the shackle itself so that the two are effectively locked together and cannot unscrew. Securing the end of the anchor line in the chain locker prevents the end of the line disappearing overboard when you let go the anchor. This securing of the end of the line should be at least as strong as the line itself, otherwise when you let go the anchor you may find the line runs out of control, and with such force that it could easily snap a light lashing. (Bear in mind, though, that you may need to let go quickly in an emergency.)

ANCHORING

When you are proposing to anchor your boat the first thing to decide is *where*. For this you need to study the chart carefully because if you steam gaily into any nice spot and throw your anchor over the side you will encounter all sorts of problems. You need to know what is on the sea bed, you need to work out the wind and tide conditions, and you need to have some idea of the depth of water. The chart and your tide tables can give you most of this information.

In general, avoid rocky bottoms when anchoring because this

is poor holding ground. Also look on the chart for any signs of underwater cables which could snarl up with the anchor and be very difficult to unravel. For the same reason do not anchor too close to mooring buoys, other vessels or anything else which might have anchors, lines or chains on the sea bed.

The best type of sea bottom to anchor on is sand, where the anchor will dig in well and hold securely. Gravel bottoms are also good. Soft mud may yield too much and a rocky bottom will not give your anchor a chance to dig in properly. If you are anchoring for pleasure sand or gravel bottoms are likely to provide the type of conditions where the water is clean and suitable for swimming, etc.

When you have studied the chart and pinpointed a spot where you would like to anchor, how do you go about getting into that spot? If you have radar it is possible to measure the distance off

An automatic anchor stowage used in conjunction with an electric capstan. Such a stowage is convenient but adds to the length of the boat – an important consideration when calculating marina charges.

the land and get into the spot with a fair degree of accuracy. Alternatively, you can take bearings off the chart and come into the anchorage by measuring these bearings. However, your exact spot is not particularly critical, so the easiest way is to take the depth of water off the chart, apply the tidal corrections (see Chapter 7) and then come into the anchorage using your echo sounder. Once you are in the correct depth and you are in a spot which is clear of other craft you can drop the anchor. Once you have done so check your position to make sure there are no problems, such as nearby rocks. In making this assessment remember that the boat will swing round when the tide turns or the wind changes so leave yourself a good margin of safety.

Coming into an anchorage the boat should stem the tide or the wind so that when the anchor is let go the line or chain will lead away from the bow. If you let go the anchor with the tide underneath you the chain may lead astern across your gleaming topsides before coming tight and allowing the boat to swing round. This is not a very seamanlike manoeuvre and stemming the wind or tide is a much more practical approach.

In crowded waters you need to watch the position of your anchor and the boat to ensure that they don't interfere with other craft.

Have the anchor clear for letting go before you come into the anchorage. If you have the rope or chain on deck for letting go don't stand in a loop or bight of the chain otherwise this will come tight round your leg. With an anchor windlass you often have to lower the anchor using windlass power, although some are fitted with a brake which allows the chain to run freely. Give a touch astern on the engines when you let go the anchor so that the chain continues to pay out leading away from the bow rather than landing in a heap on top of the anchor (this could lead to the anchor becoming snarled up).

In calm conditions you should let out anchor line equivalent to about four times the depth of water at high tide but in strong tides or a fresh wind, five or six times the depth would be more appropriate because the extra line will give a more horizontal pull on the anchor and act as a spring to reduce jerks on the anchor. There is no real harm in putting more line out except that you will swing round in a wider circle and at some stage the line has to be pulled in again – this is something to consider if you have a hand operated system.

When you have enough line out let the boat drift on the line until it is tight. This helps to dig the anchor firmly into the sea bed. If you put a finger on the tight anchor line you will feel the firmness as this happens but if a juddering movement continues on the line the anchor is probably dragging. You may want to pay out more line so that it gets a better chance to grip. Again, check that there are no hazardous objects nearby.

If you are anchoring for just a casual afternoon swim there is no need to be too concerned about the holding ability of the anchor. But if you are staying overnight in an anchorage and you want to get a good night's sleep pay out a good scope of anchor chain to give yourself peace of mind. Bear in mind when doing this that at some stage during the night the tide will turn or the wind may change. You should make sure that there is enough clearance for you to swing freely without coming into contact with other boats or buoys.

You can check on your position when at anchor by finding two fixed points on shore which are in line (or nearly in line). If the relationship between the position of these two marks changes it means your boat is moving, which probably means that it is dragging its anchor. At night you may be able to find two lights to give the same type of indication but lights may be switched off later at night so they may not be reliable. An alternative is to use the guard zone on your radar to give an indication of any movement. Sometimes an electronic position finding system is fitted with a similar facility.

If you are anchoring overnight it is a wise precaution to set your alarm clock to the time when the tide turns. This is the time when trouble might occur as the boat swings so you ought to be up and about to check all is well.

Raising the anchor should be a fairly straightforward task, particularly if you have a power windlass. However, if you have been anchored for some time or if you have not been too selective in choosing your anchorage, you may find that you can haul the anchor line short but you cannot break out the anchor itself from the sea bed. The technique, if you are faced with this problem, is to get the anchor line as short as you possibly can so that it is leading vertically downwards from the bow and then give the boat a nudge ahead on the engines. The momentum of the boat should be enough to break out the anchor from the sea bed. Do this gently, however, because it can put quite a strain on the boat – the bow will dip quite alarmingly if you use too much power.

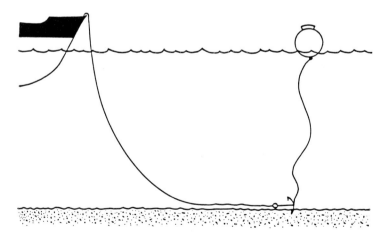

An anchor buoy can be useful to help recover the anchor but it can be a hazard to other boats.

If you suspect that the sea bed conditions may be difficult (and this type of problem usually occurs when you have been anchored for some time in hard sand) you can put an anchor buoy and line onto the anchor before you let it go. The line for the anchor buoy is fastened to the crown of the anchor where there is usually a lug fitted for the purpose. With such a line attached it is then a comparatively simple matter to steam up to the buoy, pick it up with a boat hook and haul the anchor up on this line. The success of this type of operation depends on pulling the anchor out in the reverse direction from that in which it was embedded. Anchor buoys can be a mixed blessing and it is not unknown for motor cruisers to get the line tangled in their propellers or for other boats manoeuvring nearby to foul the line.

MOORING BUOYS

In some harbours where you cannot get a berth alongside you may have to tie up to a mooring buoy. In theory, a mooring buoy is a much safer arrangement than an anchor because the buoy should be moored with a heavy weight or anchor of its own and an equally strong chain to secure it in position; these will certainly be a lot heavier than anything you might carry in the boat. However, tying up to a mooring buoy has its hazards because you are taking for granted that the moorings are in satisfactory condition and adequate for your boat. If possible get confirmation that the mooring is in sound condition and find out when it was last checked; mooring chains in harbour, particularly where there is a lot of sand and silt, have a nasty habit of wearing thin, especially in the part of the mooring called the thrash where the chain rises and falls on the bottom due to the rise and fall of tide. What might appear to be a good solid chain at the top of the mooring can be as thin as a watch chain in the area of the thrash and there will be no indication of this when you tie up to the mooring. Most responsible harbour authorities and boat yards operating moorings keep them in good condition but it does no harm to check when the mooring was last inspected.

Moorings of this type come in two forms. With the first you

simply tie up to the ring in the top of the mooring buoy using your own ropes. The best method of tying up is to put a line through the ring and bring the line back on board so that when you leave it is very easy to let go the rope and let it slip through the ring. The only thing to worry about with this type of mooring is the chafe where the rope passes through the ring. If you plan to leave the boat for any length of time some sort of chafe guard in the form of plastic tubing or rags tied round the rope will reduce the chafe. Similar protection should be placed where the rope comes on board over the bow. You should also use at least two independent ropes in case one breaks.

The second type of mooring involves picking up the buoy to find a light line or chain underneath. When you pull up this line it brings on board a heavier chain which you then make fast around your mooring post or cleats. This is a more secure type of mooring because you have a solid chain all the way down to the sea bed and there is no risk of chafe or wear and tear. You can leave a boat on this type of mooring for a considerable length of time. The only snag is that the chain is usually covered with marine growth, which can make quite a mess (and smell!) when you bring the chain on board. You also need a good fairlead or bow roller to accommodate the chain and if your bow roller is fairly shallow you may have to lash the chain in place here to prevent it jumping out when the boat swings with the wind or the tide. You will also need a good sized mooring post to make the chain fast.

Mooring buoys can often be placed in the more exposed parts of harbours and in strong winds the boat or the mooring can be subject to rather nasty sea conditions. If you leave your boat on this type of mooring, therefore, make sure that everything is secure on board.

In any form of mooring, whether anchoring or tying up to a mooring buoy, the arrangement is only as strong as its weakest link, which is often the mooring post or cleats fitted to the boat. On some modern planing motor cruisers there is a tendency to fit cleats on either side of the foredeck on the assumption that the boat will only be mooring up alongside in a marina. This type of cleat is generally not adequate for securing moorings where a single chain provides the only security. If you are going to put your boat on a mooring on a permanent basis a good strong mooring bollard forward is an essential requirement. The same applies if the boat is going to be anchored on anything except a very temporary basis. A good strong mooring bollard forward should be an essential piece of equipment on all motor cruisers because, apart from anchoring or mooring, you may need to be towed at some time and a strong bollard provides the securing point for the tow. It is not unknown for cleats to have been pulled out when they have been used for this type of operation so if you take your motor cruising seriously, put a good mooring bollard on your list of essentials.

If you leave your boat on a mooring or anchored overnight you will need a light to warn other boats of your presence. Many motor cruisers are now fitted with a white all round light which is permanently installed at the top of the mast for use as an anchor light. This type of light puts very little drain on your battery so there is no problem about leaving it on overnight. Anchor lights can be fitted which have an automatic switching device to switch them on when it gets dark and off at dawn to help conserve your battery. These are useful if you are leaving your boat unattended for a while. An alternative to a fixed anchor light is a small portable light which can be plugged into a socket on board and hoisted where it can be seen all round the horizon.

In theory, in daylight you should hoist a black ball to indicate that you are anchored but this is rarely done these days, since it is fairly obvious in daylight whether a motor cruiser is lying at anchor or not. However, if you suffer an engine failure coming into harbour and have to anchor in a fairway it is a wise precaution to hoist an anchor ball – a fender could be used for this on an emergency basis. You might otherwise find ships and other craft, being unaware of your predicament, bearing down on you.

TENDERS

If you anchor or use a mooring then you will almost certainly need a tender to get ashore. Commonly used these days is the inflatable tender which is versatile enough to be easily deflated and stowed in a comparatively small space but which when inflated provides an adequate (although sometimes damp) tender for getting ashore. Inflatables come in many shapes and sizes, some capable of planing when fitted with a suitable outboard, others very simple and basic and designed for rowing.

It is possible to carry a rigid tender on board many larger motor cruisers, particularly if davits are fitted across the transom so that the tender can be stowed here, rather than taking up valuable space on deck. There is a lot to be said for a rigid tender because it is less subject to wear and tear and tends to give a drier ride and provide a more stable platform when you step into it. However, the inflatable will stand up to a great deal more abuse than a rigid tender and its built-in fendering makes it attractive. The small rigid inflatable can be a good compromise.

Even inflatable tenders can be stowed on transom davits, this type of stowage arrangement being very attractive for motor cruisers of 25 feet (8 metres) and upwards. However, bear in mind when selecting this type of stowage that, in effect, it increases your overall length which will probably mean that your marina charges will be higher. It can be difficult to adequately secure a tender on davits over the transom when the boat is at sea. Any movement introduces wear and tear on the boat and its fittings so this type of tender stowage is not always suitable for motor cruisers which are used extensively at sea on long passages. A boat stowed thus could also be an embarrassment if the sea conditions deteriorate because waves may start to hit the tender. Serious cruiser owners will opt for the inflatable tender which can be deflated and stowed in a locker below decks out of harm's way. This convenient and safe stowage compensates for the inconvenience of having to inflate the boat each time it is required for use.

If the tender is only used occasionally propulsion by oars is probably adequate and reduces the cost. However, convenience often dictates that an outboard motor is used; with davit stowage the outboard can usually be left in place on the transom of the tender, whereas if the tender is stowed below decks then stowage also has to be found for the outboard. On diesel-powered motor cruisers, finding a suitable and safe stowage for the outboard fuel containers can be difficult and stowage also has to be found for the outboard. This could be a clamp arrangement placed on the rails at the stern.

Arranging and stowing a tender can be quite a problem on smaller motor cruisers. You should think seriously about the practicalities of this before making the decision as to whether to carry one and if so what type. Having a tender on board can be fun, particularly if you have children in the crew and it can greatly extend the range of your cruising activities.

7 · Basic navigation

Learning how to drive your motor cruiser is one thing, but getting it from one place to another requires new skills. The art of navigation is to give purpose and meaning and a sense of direction to your driving, so that eventually you end up at your destination. When navigating on land the way is clearly signposted but at sea the route may not be quite so obvious, and there will be fewer 'signposts'. Whilst it is possible to rely on instinct to some degree when you are at sea, you also have to do a fair amount of plotting and calculation, something which is not necessary with land navigation.

There tends to be an air of mystery about navigation but once you understand the basics, all that is needed is a little common sense. Certainly it can be difficult at times, particularly when there aren't many clues around as to where you are or where you are going, but generally speaking, provided you use common sense and apply thought to the situation, navigating a motor cruiser can be both interesting and rewarding.

The biggest requirement for a navigator is self confidence. If you have calculated correctly and plotted carefully you should be reasonably confident about where you are. It is very easy to sow seeds of doubt, and many navigators will hesitate when the accuracy of their navigation is questioned. This is not unreasonable, because to a certain extent navigation is intelligent guesswork, but in the absence of any better information you have to follow the route that your calculations tell you is the correct one.

With modern electronics much of the guesswork and skill has been taken out of navigation, and we will look at this aspect in

Chapter 8. However, even with modern electronics you still need to understand the basics of navigation. A latitude and longitude position shown by electronic equipment is meaningless until it is transferred on to a chart and can be viewed in relation to the land or other features around it. If you understand the basics of navigation you will be able to check the electronic information and therefore navigate with a great deal more confidence. After all, you are cruising for fun and relaxation, and navigation should be part of that fun rather than a cause for anxiety.

THE ESSENTIAL CHART

Initial Plotting
The chart is the focus of any navigation carried out on board. When you want to go from one place to another, the first thing to do is to obtain the appropriate chart and draw a line joining the two places. If this line takes you on a course overland you will need to adjust it, perhaps drawing two or three lines so that you link the two ports without touching land. At the departure port you may have to follow a channel before getting out into the open sea. When you arrive you may not make your landfall exactly at the destination port but at a prominent headland instead or a light vessel close by. You should adjust the line on the chart accordingly and then work out the details.

To do this you follow along the course drawn on the chart looking at all the features marked on the chart. Look first at the headlands. If there is deep water close into the headlands you can set your course close to the land. If there are rocks or shoals off the headland your course will have to be further out, and if they are not marked by a buoy you will need a good clearance, perhaps of a mile or more, to make sure that you pass clear.

Having adjusted your course to suit the headlands, check it for other dangers. Does your course take you too close to shoals or rocks? Again, if these are marked by buoys you can set your course close to them, but unmarked dangers must be given a wide clearance to allow for errors. Now look for buoys and other features that will give you a clue about your position en route. Buoys tend to be laid for big ships and with your shallow draft you may be able to pass inside them. They are a useful position check at sea; you may even decide to adjust your course to pass close to get a position check on a long run.

When you have looked at your proposed course in detail in this way and worked out what lies along or close to your track you are then ready to start considering the more detailed aspects of navigation such as tides, compass errors and position fixing. First, however, you will need more information about charts, which are the focus of all your navigation on board.

Chart Corrections
By the very nature of things, changes are occurring all the time at sea. For instance, the shape or depth of shoals may

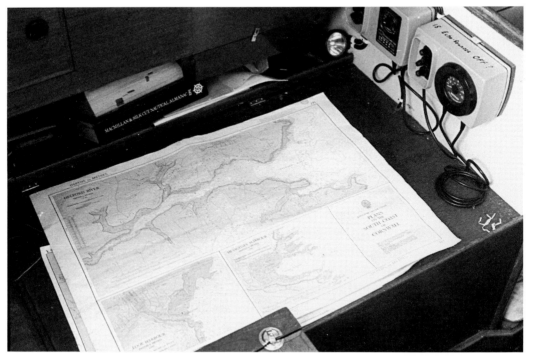

A navigation area where the chart can be laid out is useful on a motor cruiser but takes up a lot of space. The saloon table normally has to double up as the chart table.

change, navigation lights may be altered, and ships may have sunk and created wrecks. All of these changes will affect charts, and whilst you should have the latest charts on board, you should also keep these up to date by using the *Notices to Mariners*. These are published weekly to show all the changes which have taken place, and are available from the place where you buy your charts. Purchasing new charts is expensive and correcting existing charts can be a chore so there is a great temptation to take short cuts in both of these areas. You can afford to ignore many of the chart changes such as wrecks with plenty of water over them or deep water dredged channels. These will not affect your particular type of navigation. But make sure you note the essential changes on the chart, otherwise you will eventually get caught out — perhaps seeing a flashing light which you do not recognise from the chart, just at a time when you desperately need to fix your position.

Types of Chart
There are three main types of chart. First, there are general charts covering a wide area of water, and these are mainly used for planning purposes. Second, there are coastal charts, showing specific coastal areas in more detail; this is the type of chart which you will use for navigation when on passage. Third, there are harbour charts, which show the coastline and harbour channels in considerable detail; these will be used for close quarters navigation when entering or leaving harbour. With the last two types of chart, there is little room for compromise, and you must have up-to-date, fully corrected charts if you are to navigate with confidence. You can afford to keep the planning charts for longer because the changes in detail are not likely to affect your planning. In deciding which charts to carry on board, remember that if you get caught out in bad weather or encounter other problems you may have to divert from your chosen route, so it pays to have a collection of charts which extend somewhat outside your normal cruising area, just to be on the safe side.

The charts produced by hydrographic offices are designed for all types of shipping, whereas many of the more popular yachting areas are covered by specifically designed yachting charts. These have a lot to offer because often they incorporate harbour plans and tidal information all on the one sheet of paper and are thus more economic. In general, they meet most requirements, but when there is too much information on a chart some of the coastal detail is sometimes lost, which is irritating when you want to navigate inshore. The charts you eventually choose will be something of a compromise between economy and practicality.

Chart Features

When you first pick up a chart, check whether the soundings are measured in metres or in fathoms and feet. Whilst European charts use metres almost exclusively, American charts still use fathoms and feet, which could get you into trouble if you don't appreciate which is in use. Much of your navigation will be by visual identification of land features and this particularly applies on harbour approaches. Your chart carries all the information to build up a picture of the land features. You can tell from the chart whether the coastline has cliffs or sandy beaches or whether it is mud flats, even though you may never have seen it before. This is an important aspect of navigation and one which you ought to practise. It is particularly relevant when you are entering a strange harbour because your mental picture of what the harbour will look like, related to what you actually see, will give you the confidence you require to make the right approach.

Another important aspect of charts is that they show conspicuous features such as lighthouses, church spires and tall chimneys – all features which are very useful in helping to identify particular areas. They can also be useful for taking bearings to fix your position. The study of land features on the chart is an essential part of navigation, and nowhere is it more important than when you are making a landfall.

The Tools for the Job

Whilst the chart is probably the navigator's most essential tool, you also need some other equipment. A pencil and eraser are basic items – use a soft pencil so that it can be rubbed out easily. A good quality soft eraser will help to give the chart a long life.

Course lines are drawn on the chart using parallel rules. Apart from drawing straight lines, parallel rules can be lined up with lines drawn on the chart and then, by sliding one part of the rules at a time, the direction of this line can be transferred to the compass rose on the chart to discover the direction of the line. They are easy to use on a flat chart table, but can be awkward when the boat is bouncing around at sea. This has led to the development of a number of patented devices which perform much the same function as parallel rules but which can be used in a much more flexible way, allowing courses and bearings to be measured even when the chart is on an uneven surface or even when the chart is being held on your lap.

The other basic tool used for navigation are dividers, which are used for measuring distances. You simply open the dividers to span the two points whose distance apart you want to measure on the chart, and then transfer the opened dividers to the vertical scale at the side of the chart. This scale is marked in degrees and minutes of latitude; and if you have a chart which covers a large area you will notice that this latitude scale is not even. The divisions at the bottom of the scale in the Northern Hemisphere are closer together than those at the top in order to accommodate the distortion which occurs when part of the earth's surface (which is a sphere) is transferred on to a flat paper chart. In order to measure distance on this scale you must transfer the dividers to the scale adjacent to the measured line so that distances are kept in the correct proportion. When measuring distance in this way, one minute of latitude is equivalent to one nautical mile. In between the minute marks the scale is usually divided into fifths or tenths so that you can measure the decimal parts of a mile.

Parallel rules and dividers are also used to transfer latitude and longitude to and from the chart. This is necessary for entering information into electronic position finding equipment or vice versa and it is achieved by the simple expedient of measuring from one of the fixed lattice lines on the chart to the point of interest, and then transferring this to the appropriate scale at the side or the bottom of the chart, depending on whether you are measuring latitude or longitude and taking off the reading on the appropriate scale. This identifies the position by latitude and longitude co-ordinates and is mainly used when transferring positions between the chart and electronic instruments.

COMPASS COURSES

The line you draw on the chart represents your course and when you have measured its direction using the parallel rules this is known as the true course. The compass you have on the boat, however, is a magnetic compass and to find the correct course to *steer* you have to apply corrections for variation and deviation.

Variation
Variation is a correction applied to compensate for the fact that the compass points to magnetic north rather than true north. The figures for variation in your vicinity can be found on the chart, usually at the centre of the compass rose. These are given in degrees; you simply add them to or subtract them from the true course to arrive at your *compass* course. The variation can be either to the east or west, and if you learn the rhyme *Error east, compass least – error west, compass best* you will remember that an easterly variation has to be subtracted from a true course because as the error is *east*, the compass is *least* and is therefore a *lower* figure than the true course. A westerly variation would be added. (When it comes to translating compass courses into true courses the reverse applies.)

Deviation
The second correction for the compass is deviation and is much more complex to calculate. Deviation is caused by magnetic influences on the boat itself such as the steel of the engine, or magnets in loudspeakers – in fact any iron or steel fittings around the boat. These all exert a magnetic influence which can pull the compass needle one way or the other away from its

proper heading, and you have to allow for these influences.

The deviation is found by 'swinging' the boat, which is usually a job for a compass adjuster. The boat is turned through a full circle and the compass adjuster takes readings on a selection of headings; from this he can work out the deviation. He will also check that the compass is properly aligned with the fore and aft line of the boat, and if he finds any major errors these can be corrected or at least reduced by fitting compensating magnets alongside the compass. Correcting a compass in this way is quite a skilled job and is something that should be done every year or two to maintain compass accuracy. Once the compass has been corrected you must then make sure that you don't introduce any further errors by placing any magnetic material near it. This is not just a question of looking around the wheelhouse to see whether you might have left a knife or other such object close to the compass; remember that magnetic influence can pass through GRP or wood, so you must look on the other side of the bulkhead, too, to see what might be close to the compass inside the cabin.

When the compass adjuster has done his job you will have a card showing the error on different headings, and these will be marked east or west. They are applied using the same rule as for variation to find the compass course. Once you have applied variation and deviation you can relate the courses on the chart to the compass on the boat.

Steering Compass
You will use your steering compass a great deal so take care of it. Go for the largest compass you can fit or afford. Fast boats require a compass with heavy damping to stop the card swinging about too much when the boat is moving. Mount the compass as far forward of the steering position as you reasonably can so that you don't have to refocus too much from looking through the wheelhouse windows down to the compass and back again. Night time lighting on the compass is important and you usually have a choice between red or white lighting simply by changing the bulb. A dimmer incorporated into the lighting is a useful feature so that you can adjust it to suit the conditions.

Hand Bearing Compasses

Hand bearing compasses are not used a great deal on motor cruisers nowadays largely because of the advent of electronic position fixing systems. However, a hand bearing compass is a useful back up, partly to find out where you are if your electronics fail, but also to provide a back up if something should go wrong with the steering compass. You can't correct the hand bearing compass for deviation because you may use it in several different parts of the boat, so the answer is to use it in a position which is as far away from any magnetic influence as possible, so that there is no deviation to take into account. But you must still apply variation wherever you use this compass to produce true bearings for the chart.

Steering Bias

Applying corrections to the course for deviation and variation are only part of the story. You will find that no matter who steers the boat they will invariably introduce bias to the course they should be steering. This bias could have quite an effect on the course you make good, i.e. the course that you actually achieve, and the only way to find out if there is a bias is to watch the steering for a while and then estimate what the bias is. Overall it is unlikely to be more than 5 degrees. Normally you will find that if the wind is on the beam the helmsman steers away from the wind. The answer is to apply a correction to the course in the opposite direction to counteract the bias, or to steer by autopilot.

Tides

Tides can affect much more noticeably the course which is steered. In trying to follow the line that you drew on the chart you will have to apply corrections to allow for the way the tidal stream or currents set the boat away from the desired course. If there were no tide or currents to take into account your course through the water would be the same as a course over ground. Since the water is moving, the bow of the boat has to be pointed into the flow to counteract the undesired movement away from the course.

Currents will always flow in the same direction and can be

quite strong, as in the Gulf Stream off Florida. As for tides, both their strength and direction can be found from tidal atlases. There are usually 12 of these charts to a series (i.e. for an area) each chart covering a period of an hour throughout the 12-hour cycle between one high water and the next. The tide will generally set in one direction for 6 hours and then reverse direction for the next 6 hours. The strength of the tide is much less consistent however, reaching a peak half way through the tide and dropping away to nothing as the tide turns.

Tides are never consistent because each month there are spring tides and neap tides. Spring tides are the higher tides, when obviously more water has to flow past a given point and therefore the tidal stream is stronger. Neap tides are weaker and so the tidal flow will be much less. In tidal atlases there are usually two numbers alongside the direction arrows indicating the rate of tidal flow in knots; the higher of these is the flow of spring tides, whilst the lower relates to neaps. You will have to interpolate between these two figures to work out the rate of flow for any time in between.

To use the tidal atlas first find the time of high water for a particular day from the tide tables. By looking at the heights of the tides in the tide tables you can also find out if the tide on a particular day is a spring or a neap tide or somewhere in between. This will give you the information to work out what the strength of the tidal flow will be. Each chart in the tidal atlas is marked in hours *before* or *after* high water so that you can find the appropriate chart which will show the way the tides will be flowing at that time.

In general tidal streams run up and down the coastline, so when you are making a coastal passage you can generally assume that the tide will either be running with you or against you. This makes the job of applying the tidal corrections to your navigation much simpler. There will be distortions in this flow, however, particularly around headlands, in estuaries and bays. You should study the tidal atlases quite carefully to make sure that the tide will not set you into danger. The tide will obviously have a much greater effect on a slower boat than a fast one because the speed of the tide in relation to the speed of the boat will be much greater. On a planing motor cruiser the effect of the tide is much reduced but you must still take it into account, particularly if you are motoring across the tide because it can still affect your course by up to 5 degrees or more.

You will want to apply a correction for the tide to your course line on the chart unless it is directly ahead or astern. First, work out roughly how long it will take you to make the passage at an average speed and then draw the proposed course line on each page of the tidal atlas, marking the boat's position at the appropriate time for the tide. Thus, if you leave at 1000 hrs, you will want the first position after an hour to be on the tidal atlas chart which refers to 1100 hrs.

From these positions you will then be able to see each hour how the tide will affect the boat. On any passage, the tide will normally set first one way and then the reverse. This means that if you add the tidal set in one direction and then the other, you can deduct the larger from the smaller to find the overall effect of the tide. The direction will be that of the larger figure.

Having calculated the distance and direction of the tidal effect, draw a line on the chart in the reverse direction (remember, you want to counteract the tide) from the far end of the line, i.e. your destination point. Along this line mark off a distance equivalent to the overall set of the tide (measure from the scale at the side of the chart), and join this point with your starting point on your course line. The direction of this new line from your starting point will be the course you want to steer to counteract the tide – but remember that the compass corrections still have to be applied to this course before you can use it on your steering compass.

It sounds complicated, but as you get used to working the tides you will be able to do much of the calculation in your head and will be able to make your tidal corrections quite quickly. But in the early stages it is best to do the calculations the long way.

HEIGHT OF TIDE

On the chart, the depths shown are those of chart datum which can usually be taken as a level below which the tide seldom falls.

It is much more precisely defined than that, but for practical purposes, chart datum can be assumed to be the level of the lowest of low waters. Working on the safe side, tidal corrections are added to these depths to find out how much water there will be at a particular point at a particular time. When a sandbank is shown to dry out at low water on the chart, for example, the height at which the bank dries has to be subtracted from the height of the tide to obtain the amount of water which may be over that bank at any particular time.

The tide tables show the height and time of both high and low water for each tide. The height figures for the tide will vary from day to day and if you look at the tables you will notice that there is a progressive increase or decrease in the heights. The high water figures get higher and the low waters get lower as the tides move towards springs; the reverse happens when they move towards neap tides.

The tide does not rise and fall at the same rate throughout the whole period of a tide. The water rises slowly at first, then quickens at the middle of a tide and then slows again near high water. A very good guide to measuring this variation in rise and fall is as follows. If you divide the rise of the tide, that is the height between low water and high water, into 12ths, the tide rise is 1/12th in the first hour, 2/12ths in the second hour, 3/12ths in the third hour, and 3/12ths in the fourth hour. In the fifth hour the rate of rise then drops to 2/12ths again, with 1/12th in the sixth hour.

When you want to work out the height of the tide at any particular time, take the nearest high water and low water heights and subtract the height of low water from that of high water to find the range of tide. Now divide this figure by 12 and you have the basis for working out the tides as above. For instance, if you want to find the rise in the first hour after low water, this will be 1/12th of the range, which you then add on to the height of low water. If you want to find the rise of the tide after 3 hours, this will be 1/12th for the first hour, plus 2/12ths for the second hour and 3/12ths for the third hour, making a total of 6/12ths. When you add this on to the height of low water you obtain the height of the tide at that particular time.

Example:

Height of high water	3.6 metres
Height of low water	1.2 metres
Range of tide	2.4 metres
Divide by 12	0.2 metres
Height of tide at 3 hours flood	0.2×3 (3/12ths) = 0.6 metres
Height of tide above chart datum	$1.2 + 0.6$ = 1.8 metres

Of course this system only gives you the height of the tide every hour between high water and low water, but for most practical purposes this time span is adequate and the chances are that you won't be cutting your depth margins any finer than that. With experience you can start to work out these tidal corrections in your head using approximations and unless you are working to very critical limits this will usually be adequate.

Tides are one of the most complex areas of navigation and so far we have assumed that the tide rises and falls in a 12-hour cycle. In some areas this is not always the case – the tidal stream may, for instance, flow for 8 hours and ebb for only 4 hours. Then again, the time for high water doesn't always correspond with the time at which the tidal stream changes direction, or the tide may hold up at high water for a longer period and not follow the regular pattern we have assumed to exist in the calculations above.

These tidal idiosyncrasies are usually mentioned in the tide tables and it pays to study these and the tidal atlases carefully and to get to know and understand them well. In many boating areas tides have a tremendous influence on what you can and can't do. They also affect the sea conditions when for example the wind is against the tide, and because of their importance it should become a habit before you go to sea to check on the tides throughout your route. This should only take a few minutes but it is time well spent. A note pad listing the times of tide can be very useful and saves you having to rely on your memory.

FIXING YOUR POSITION

Knowing your position is probably one of the most important pieces of information you can have as a navigator. Once you have fixed your position you have a point on which to base all your other calculations. With the advent of electronic position fixing, visual position fixing is becoming a dying art, but it should not be overlooked because no navigator worth his salt relies entirely on electronics. Even when your electronic equipment is in perfect working order it is good to have the reassurance of being able to fix your position by other means.

Position Lines
The basis of all position fixing is the position line. This is not your course line, but a line drawn on the chart somewhere along which lies your position. A position line could be half a mile long, or 100 miles long, it doesn't really matter, as long as you know that your position is somewhere along that line. The position line doesn't even have to be a straight line. It may be curved if it is a range from a fixed point on land. Or it may even be a squiggly line following a sounding contour if you know, for instance, that you have just crossed the 10 metre line. One position line will not give you a fix, but the point where two position lines cross provides the fix to show exactly where you are.

The secret of position fixing, therefore, is to obtain position lines. There are many ways in which this can be done. Latitude and longitude are position lines and are the standard means of identifying a position on a chart, but there is no easy way of measuring latitude and longitude except by astro-navigation or electronic position fixing systems. Alternative means of providing position lines are by taking compass bearings from identifiable objects on shore, or transit bearings or using sounding lines. Your actual course line can be a position line of sorts, although its accuracy might be slightly dubious!

The simplest type of position fixing is achieved by taking bearings with a hand bearing compass. It requires a little

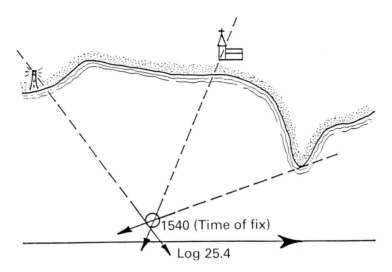

1540 (Time of fix)

Log 25.4

Fixing the position by means of cross bearings taken with a hand bearing compass.

practice to use a compass for taking bearings, particularly at night (and remember to keep the compass away from magnetic influence). Finding a suitable point from which to take bearings is not always easy either. Lighthouses and lightships are obvious starting points because they are readily identifiable both on the chart and on the coastline. Headlands can also be useful, particularly where they have a clear cut edge, but you can also use hills, mountains, church spires, tall chimneys, water towers, piers and even wrecks. It doesn't really matter what objects you use for taking bearings provided you can see and identify them to take a bearing and can also identify them confidently on the chart.

You have to be a little careful sometimes with hills and even headlands because confusion can arise and it is very easy to make assumptions about what you see without getting a really positive identification.

At least two bearings are necessary to get a fix, but with only two you have no real check; three bearings are a much more satisfactory way of fixing the position. It is very rare that these three bearings will cross at exactly the same point when you have applied the corrections for variation and deviation and plotted them on the chart, but with any luck they will be in close proximity in what is called a 'cocked hat'. You can assume that you are in the centre of the triangle formed by the crossing of the three bearings. Soundings could help to check the position.

NAVIGATING BY EYE

Text books on navigation will offer other ways of fixing your position, such as taking running fixes and doubling the angle on the bow. In 40 years of navigation, I have never used these methods – they suffer from the big disadvantage of fixing your position when you are off a headland rather than before you get to it, and their accuracy can leave much to be desired. Navigating by eye is a practical approach to navigation. In modern motor cruiser navigation it is rare to use a hand bearing compass let alone these complicated position fixing methods.

In clear weather you can do much of your navigation by eye, setting up a course to the next headland simply by lining up the bow of the boat to pass outside the headland bearing in mind that the tide may set you inshore. Similarly you can navigate through buoyed channels by eye. This type of casual navigation is fine provided you relate what you are doing to what is shown on the chart. You should also make a note of the time you pass any navigation mark such as a buoy or a headland, as well as noting your course and speed. From this information you will have a reference point for dead reckoning (see later) if visibility closes in.

Navigating by eye is perfectly OK if there are no dangers off the headlands, or sandbanks or rocks close to your course. With practice you can estimate the distance off a headland with a fair degree of accuracy, and this will be adequate to fix your position in most situations. If there are dangers such as rocks or shallow water close to your proposed course then you may want to adjust your course to give a wider margin for errors. Of course, if you have radar or electronic position fixing equipment you can use this to supplement your 'eyeball' navigation. This also helps to build up the neccessary experience and confidence quickly.

At night eyeball navigation is not so easy and it is much harder to judge distances. Generally at night headlands and shoals should be given a wider margin anyway, and a hand bearing compass can be useful to help fix your position. Soundings are another method of fixing, or at least checking, your position. A sudden change in the depth lines shown on the chart will show up clearly on the echo sounder and will help to confirm a position – and often the depth shown on the sounder will give a good indication of the distance offshore. Before making too many assumptions from the soundings, check carefully on the chart to make sure that there are not similar areas close by where the same indications on the sounder would occur.

Dead Reckoning
Dead reckoning is used for navigation when you are out of sight of land, either on a long, open sea crossing or perhaps when visibility is bad. This method makes use of the line which you first drew on the chart, but instead of working out where you are going, you do the reverse, working out where you are by measuring off the course you have steered, the distance you have travelled and the effect of the tide upon that course.

The course is from the compass so it has to be corrected by applying the variation and deviation before you have a true course to lay off on the chart. The speed is obtained from the log (or you can use the engine rpm), relating these to the speed and then multiplying by the time to find the distance travelled. The point on the course line where the distance run intersects is called the *dead reckoning position*, but you will also want to take into account the effect of the tide to get the boat's position. From the DR position a line is laid off in the direction in which the tide has set (this might be a combination of two opposite directions as when counteracting the tide) and along this line you measure off the distance the tide has set over the full period of time. The resulting spot is where the boat should be and is called the *estimated position.*

It is a test of any navigator's skill to compare his estimated position with the actual position, if this can be ascertained. With practice you will get better at estimating the effect of the tides, the helmsman's bias and even the wind. The effect of the wind is generally very small on a motor cruiser but a fresh wind on the beam can blow the boat off course by a degree or two so in

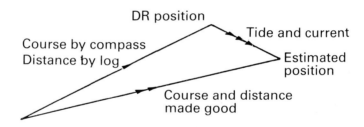

Plotting the vector triangle for dead reckoning. The estimated position worked out this way should coincide with a fix if you could get one, but helmsman's bias could introduce an error into the course steered by compass.

these conditions altering the course a couple of degrees into the wind can help.

SIGNPOSTS AT SEA

One of the simplest and most obvious ways of fixing your position at sea is to be close alongside a buoy or lightship whose position you can identify on the chart. It doesn't take any measurement to work out where you are in these circumstances. These buoys and other navigational marks form the signposts at sea which help to simplify navigation and give reassurance. They are used to mark sandbanks, shoals, and isolated rocks and wrecks, all of which present dangers for a navigator, but in all except small harbours buoyage is there to help large ships rather than small motor cruisers. This means that the buoys marking a channel into a harbour entrance are placed to mark the deep water areas. There can be plenty of shallow water which is navigable by shallow draft motor cruisers and which can enable you to make short cuts. However, when you take these short cuts don't cut the margins too fine because the areas outside the buoyed channels are not always surveyed to the same degree of accuracy.

Information about buoys and lights is shown clearly on charts and once you understand the shorthand way in which they are labelled, a whole host of information becomes available. In the daytime it is the colour of the buoy, its shape and the name on its side which identify it. The colour and shape can be seen at some distance whilst the name can only be read when you are close to it. At night the characteristics of the flashing light identify the buoy. It thus forms a very positive way of identifying your position. The standard international system has the starboard hand buoys painted green and port hand buoys red. This is the relevant colour scheme when you are entering harbour. When leaving harbour the colours will obviously be reversed. Buoy lights follow the same pattern, being red on the red buoys and green on the green buoys. In the USA, the colour schemes are reversed and the phrase 'red, right, return' helps to remind you. Take nothing for granted, therefore, and always check the chart.

In addition to these channel buoys the international system uses black and yellow buoys to identify isolated shoals, wrecks or middle grounds. These buoys are all the same shape but have different colour combinations. They are identified in the daytime by two triangular topmarks. If both of the triangle points are pointing upwards the buoy is marking the north side of the danger area; if the two points are pointing downwards the buoy is on the south side of the danger. Buoys to the west have the tips of the cones pointing towards one another, and those on the east side have their tips pointing away from one another. The golden rule with all these buoys is that you pass them to seaward on the side they indicate, in other words you pass to the north of a north indicating buoy and to the south of a south indicating buoy. All buoyage is virtually self explanatory in terms of which side you have to pass and how you have to navigate through an area, but in all cases it makes sense to refer to the positions of the buoys on the chart.

There are also isolated danger marks, which have two black spheres one above the other; the buoys themselves are black with red horizontal bands. You may pass either side of these marks, but common sense dictates that you do not sail too close to them because they are mounted on the danger they are warning you about.

These are the type of marks you will find at sea and in the approaches to main ports and harbours. They are costly to maintain, however, and in many small ports the buoys marking the approach channels may not have lights. Once you are in the harbour you may also find that the channels are marked by sticks or other very simple marking systems, the significance of which you have to find out locally by referring to detailed charts of the harbour concerned. The markings of the channels may not always be as reliable as one would wish, so in these situations it is advisable to use your echo sounder and to keep your eyes peeled.

Out at sea, buoys are generally few and far between unless the shoals or dangers extend a long way offshore. Along the coastlines you will often find buoys marking patches of rocks or shoals, whilst the main approaches to major ports or significant danger areas will often be marked by light vessels, very large buoys called Lanby, or in some cases fixed light towers. Lighthouses can also be found offshore where there are isolated rocks above water level, but in general lighthouses are on land where they serve more as a guide for position fixing than for indicating dangers, although at night their flashing lights are a reassuring warning of the location of significant headlands.

These 'signposts' of the sea form the basis of the most simple form of navigation, i.e. they warn us about potential dangers, but you cannot assume that because of these warnings the rest of the sea is free from danger. Navigating a motor cruiser involves putting all the different information together, whether from buoys, bearings or electronic fixing positions, checking one against the other and assessing the results.

NAVIGATION IN FOG

Fog or poor visibility represents the greatest challenge to any navigator, because many of the traditional methods of navigation are not possible in these conditions. Electronics, in the form of radar and position fixing systems, can take a great deal of the nightmare out of fog, but even with these systems available your navigation has to take on a new and sharper edge. Your planning and plotting, too, have to be geared to the new conditions.

Fog signals are a notoriously unreliable method of fixing your position in poor visibility, although they can give warning of your approaching dangers if you hear them. Because of the engine noise on a motor cruiser you are unlikely to hear fog signals until you are very close, and certainly they should not be relied upon. Dead reckoning is a very important method of navigating in fog and is certainly a means of making progress in open water, but problems arise when you want to make a landfall.

Landfalls

To make a landfall you need to choose a stretch of coastline with no off-lying dangers which you can approach with safety. This stretch of coastline should be as long as possible, perhaps 5 miles or more, so that even if there are errors in your navigation there are still safety margins to accommodate these errors as you make your approach. Ideally, the coastline should have a gently shelving area in front of it so that you will have some warning of your approach on the echo sounder as the depth decreases. In this way you can make your landfall with a fair degree of confidence – but keep your eyes glued to the echo sounder and your hand on the throttles ready to stop. In these conditions try to approach the coastline at an angle, rather than straight on, so that if you do see something suddenly coming out of the fog,

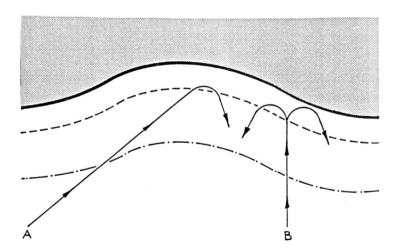

A   B

It is much better to approach a coastline at a shallow angle as in A, so that when the sounding decreases you know which way to turn for safety. A direct approach as in B leaves you with two options and a much larger angle to turn through.

there will be only one obvious way to turn out to seaward, and you won't have to turn through such a large angle to avoid the danger.

This technique can also be used when you are coasting in poor visibility and trying to find a headland. Rather than set a course directly for the end of the headland, you should set a course for a point some way inside the headland, sure in the knowledge that you will sight land ahead and not disappear past the headland without sighting it at all. Again you should check on the chart to make sure that there are no nasty off-lying rocks or other such dangers inside the headland.

One of the hardest things to find in poor visibility is an isolated buoy or lightship which marks the approach to a harbour. This requires pinpoint accuracy and is never easy if there are strong tides running. It may be simpler to make a landfall on a stretch of coastline first, or to use some other feature to help fix your position so that you shorten the distance between your last fix and finding the lightship. The shorter the distance, the more accurate your position is likely to be.

In fog your tactics will depend a great deal on the geography of the area; study the chart very carefully and try to visualise not only where you wish to make your landfall, but what you may encounter in the way of hazards if you miss your landfall point and overshoot. This is where experience really begins to tell, so practise the techniques in fine weather and you will feel a lot more comfortable when the fog comes down.

It is not only fixing your position which is important in foggy conditions; you also have to concern yourself with other craft in the vicinity. One rule you should always follow is that your speed should allow you to stop within at least half of the visibility range.

We will look again at some of the techniques for navigating in fog in the next chapter when we consider the use of radar.

8 · Electronics

Electronics have made a great difference to motor cruiser navigation. Modern electronics provide a read-out of your latitude and longitude at all times, a display of the coastline and other vessels around you, and, to a certain extent, a picture of what is going on underwater. Electronics take a great deal of the guesswork out of navigation, making it a much more precise art. The navigator still needs to have his wits about him, however, because although the information may be presented in a very precise way, this very preciseness can be misleading. Indeed, one of the disturbing features of modern electronics is the way that information is presented with very little indication of its inherent accuracy.

Before electronics, navigators had to find their position by the interpretation of a number of different factors, so that, having established their position, they had a fair idea of its level of accuracy. With modern electronics very little interpretation is required – it is difficult to argue with an electronic read-out! As a motor cruiser owner you need to understand something about electronics and the accuracy of different systems in order to appreciate the validity of the information they give.

WAYPOINT NAVIGATION

Before electronics, positions at sea were almost invariably given by a means of bearing and distance from a fixed point on land. However, electronics give you a position determined by latitude and longitude, and from this has developed a whole new system of navigation called *waypoint navigation*.

Latitude and longitude on their own are quite meaningless; no more than just a jumble of figures. They only have meaning when you put them on a chart. They will then indicate a position which can be related to the course which you plan to follow. Waypoint navigation involves drawing lines on the chart in the same way as discussed in Chapter 7. When you want to alter course you read the latitude and longitude of that position. These positions are then fed into the Decca, Loran or Satnav equipment as waypoints and from that stage the electronics will be able to show you the course and distance to the next waypoint, the distance that you are to one side or other of your required track, the speed and distance being made good, i.e. over the ground and of course the latitude and longitude of your current position.

You may be overwhelmed by the amount of information being presented to you, but the most important information to remember in waypoint navigation is the course and distance to the next waypoint, and the cross track error, which indicate where you are in relation both to the next waypoint and to the course which you want to follow. From this information you can decide whether you ought to alter course to bring the boat back onto its desired track or whether you are happy going along as you are. If the cross track error puts you to one side or other of the required track it is important to relate this to the chart to make sure that your deviation from the chosen track has not taken you close to any hazards.

With most position finding systems you can feed a series of waypoints into the instrument to form a route. Provided you have programmed the route correctly, as you approach one waypoint the instrument will automatically switch to the next waypoint. You therefore have continuing information about the track you are following. It is possible to link position finding systems into the autopilot so that even these course alterations are perfomed automatically. However, the manual interface provides a useful check on navigation – it is not a good idea to rely too much on a fully automatic system because you do not have a fully automatic look-out to match; you still need to keep your eyes open.

The advantage of waypoint navigation is that all the planning and most of the work can be done in harbour. It is less likely that you will make mistakes under these conditions, and with the position finding receiver fully programmed you will be well prepared if you encounter bad weather. On a fast motor cruiser where it may be difficult or even impossible to carry out plotting on a chart when you are underway, electronic waypoint navigation becomes one of the few practical ways of carrying out precise navigation. Always keep the chart close at hand for easy reference and don't let the boat drift too far off the proposed track.

RADAR NAVIGATION

Radar can also be used to fix your position at sea electronically. With radar it is possible to measure off both ranges and bearings from identifiable features along the coastline. However,

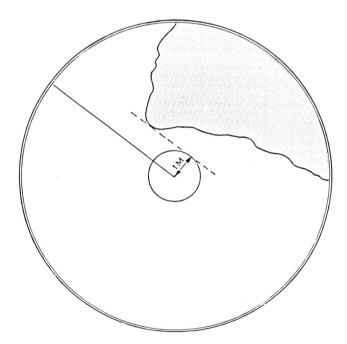

Radar display – range ring set to pass 1 mile off headland

Using the heading line and range ring on the radar to gauge the distance you will pass off a headland.

bearings are not particularly reliable when taken from a radar because these are only relative bearings, i.e. they relate to the bow of the boat and not to the compass.

To obtain a compass bearing you have to apply the boat's compass heading to the relative bearing, which means reading the compass at the same time as you take the bearing. This can lead to inaccuracies if the boat is swinging. Ranges are much more reliable when taken off the radar as you don't have to apply any corrections and can simply transfer them straight to the chart. A pair of compasses is ideal for laying off these ranges. With practice it is possible to plot ranges and fix your position even when you don't have a flat chart table available. If your motor cruiser has both radar and an electronic position finding system, plotting radar ranges in this way can be a useful check on what the electronic position finding systems are telling you.

There is another radar technique which is similar to waypoint navigation. When you have identified the headland around which you want to alter course to pass, say, one mile off, by setting the variable range marker to one mile you can adjust the heading of the boat until the heading line is approximately one mile off the headland. This will give you a check on your heading and distance off. Do remember though that by setting the course in this way no allowance has been made for tide, so if you find the clearance between the proposed course and the headland decreasing, you will know that the tide is setting you in and you must adjust course accordingly.

Radar can be a particularly effective navigation tool in narrow channels, provided of course that the buoyage or other navigation marks can be identified on the screen. With the heading marker lined up on the channel you have a good guide to your future direction, but always back up the radar information with visual observations when you can. The echo sounder which indicates the depth of water can also be used to confirm the position.

POSITION FIXING SYSTEMS

The three main position fixing systems which are likely to be found on a motor cruiser are Decca (not available in the US),

Loran and satellite navigation. Decca and Loran are hyperbolic navigation systems which use transmissions from shore-based stations to produce position lines from which the boat's position can be fixed. Satellite navigation uses signals from special navigation satellites which, when analysed and processed in the receiver, enable the position to be determined. The hyperbolic navigation systems tend to be comparatively short-range, Decca only being effective up to 300 or 400 miles from the transmitters and Loran perhaps up to 1,000 miles, whereas satellite navigation is worldwide in coverage.

Decca and Loran
With Decca and Loran a chain of stations, comprising a master and two or three slave or secondary stations, transmit signals according to a very precisely timed sequence. With the Decca system the onboard receiver measures the difference in phase between signals received from a master transmitting station and a slave, or secondary, transmitter to give a position line. A similar measurement from a second pair of stations gives a second position line to produce a fix. With Loran the onboard receiver measures the time difference (TD) between the received signals from different pairs of stations to produce a fix. These navigation systems are described as hyperbolic because that is the shape of the position lines when plotted on the chart.

With the early types of receiver it was necessary to use special charts with hyperbolic position lines overprinted. Modern receivers are computerised and translate the positions

A typical pattern of hyperbolic position lines formed between two Loran transmitters, master and secondary. The lines are identified by the time difference numbers. The position lines are closest along the baseline to give a more accurate position fix. In the area of the baseline extension a large change in the boat's position would produce only a very small change in the Loran reading, so position fixes here are very unreliable.
A similar pattern of lines is produced between the master and another secondary transmitter. The boat's position is shown by the intersection of the lines from the two pairs of transmitters. Decca transmitters form a similar pattern, but measure the phase difference instead.

generated by the hyperbolic position lines into latitude and longitude positions, and these are shown on the screen. The latitude and longitude position given should be treated with some caution because accuracy can vary quite considerably.

For greatest accuracy the position lines should cross almost at

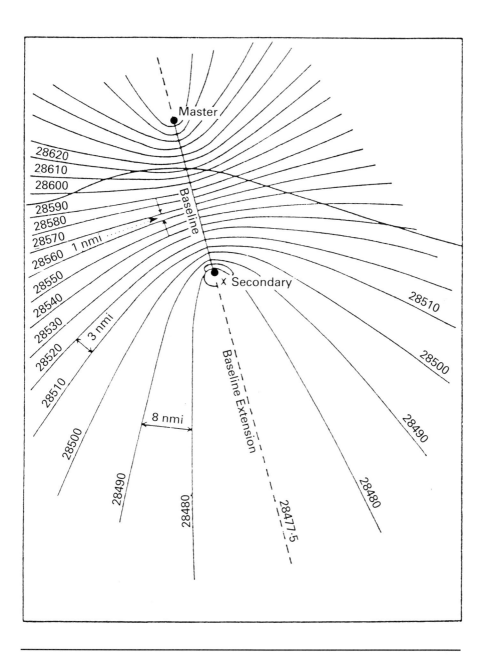

right angles. If the crossing angle is shallow a small error in one position line will have a pronounced effect on the final position. This tends to occur towards the extremity of the range when you are normally well clear of land so it may not be too significant, but with modern receivers which automatically switch from one chain to the next as you progress along the coast you may find yourself working at extreme ranges without realising it.

Another problem can occur even when you are quite close to one of the transmitting stations; you could find yourself on what is known as the 'baseline extension'. This is a line joining the master transmitter and a secondary. Along or close to this line positions are generally unreliable. The answer to all of these problems is to have a chart of the various transmitting stations and the chain patterns of signals on board so that you are aware of potential errors.

There may also be reduced accuracy at night, particularly at dawn and dusk. However, these potential problems and errors should not dissuade you from using this equipment. Both Decca and Loran can produce excellent positions with an accuracy of a quarter of a mile or better, and they can produce these positions in fog and bad weather when you might find it very difficult to get any other position fixing information. The valuable information obtainable from Decca and Loran is a great advance on many alternative methods of navigation, provided you remember to check your position by other means whenever you get the chance. If you are making a landfall or approaching any other area of potential danger, always use your echo sounder or have some other form of double check available.

Satellite Navigation
There are two types of satellite navigation, Transit Satnav which has been in existence now for a number of years and is well established, and Navstar GPS which is a brand new system scheduled to be fully operational by 1990.

Transit Satnav obtains information from satellites which are in polar orbit. The position is established by measuring the frequency changes as a single satellite passes overhead. These measurements can establish the position with an excellent degree of accuracy, down to 100 yards or even better, but they

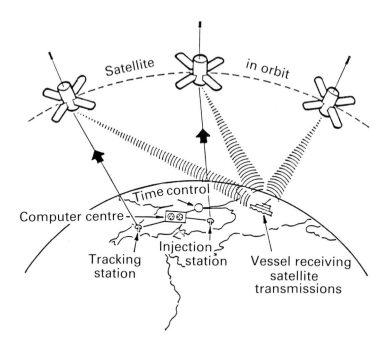

The basics of the Transit satellite system.

are very dependent on accurate course and speed being fed into the receiver. The speed is particularly important because this will affect the frequency changes. A 1 knot error in speed, especially when you are on an easterly or westerly course, could perhaps produce a position inaccuracy of up to a quarter of a mile in higher latitudes. It is normal to connect the log to the Satnav receiver but for greatest accuracy an allowance for the tide or current should also be included. On a fast motor cruiser the speed input by log may not be very accurate, allowing larger errors to creep in.

Another factor which has to be taken into account with this system is that the satellites only pass overhead every 60–90 minutes, so you only get a position fix at these intervals. In between, the log and compass inputs will carry out a form of automatic dead reckoning for you. This time interval of fix may be suitable for a slow boat during coastal navigation, but for a fast motor cruiser it is inadequate as you may have travelled 30 miles or more between fixes. For fast boats, Decca or Loran is a much better proposition, but Transit Satnav can provide a useful alternative on slower motor cruisers.

Navstar GPS, when it becomes operational, is likely to make all the other position fixing systems obsolete. When the full constellation of 21 satellites is available this system will give continuous position fixing with a very high degree of accuracy, generally in the order of 100 yards, and it will not be influenced by weather conditions. For the first time a highly accurate worldwide position fixing system will be available. Initially, though, the receivers are likely to be considerably more expensive than those used in other systems. It may be five years or more before we see low-cost receivers coming onto the market, bringing the system into general use.

Because of its complete worldwide coverage and its high accuracy, Navstar GPS will be suitable for coastal and open water passages, and even for harbour navigation in certain circumstances. It is very much the system of the future, and whilst it may make the other position fixing systems redundant, it is likely that Loran and, possibly, Decca will be retained to provide an alternative system of position fixing and/or checking in many of the popular boating areas.

Radar

With modern, small boat units, radar can be fitted in virtually any motor cruiser. It is a wonderful piece of equipment, providing you with your position, drawing a map of the land around you, and it can also show you other vessels nearby.

It all sounds too good to be true – and the problem is that radar never quite tells you the whole story. However, it does give you a great deal of useful information, and if you are to use that information intelligently you need to have a good idea of how radar works, and what it can and can't do.

Unlike other motor cruiser electronics, there are certain pieces of information that have to be coaxed out of the radar set. The user should know the area he is working in and he should be able to identify images on the radar screen. With the map-like display of radar it is very easy to take what you see at face value and to assume that it is a bird's eye view of the area around you. However, the radar is not looking down over the area; it is looking out from a position not much higher than your own eyes. If you turn round through 360 degrees standing on board you will get some idea of what the radar is seeing. Radar has one big advantage over your eyes, however, and that is its ability to measure distance so that its horizontal viewpoint can be translated into a plan-like display. This is not the same as a map

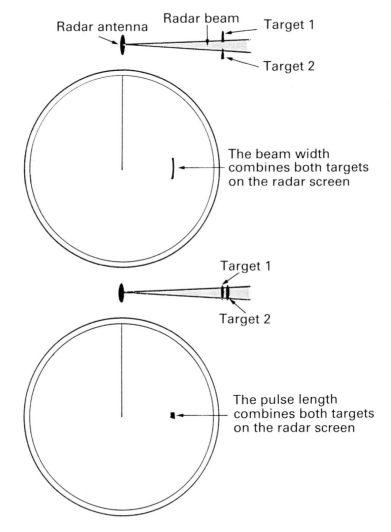

TOP: *A wide beam width on the radar will encompass two targets in the one beam and they will show up as a single elongated echo on the screen.*

BOTTOM: *Two targets on the same bearing can be encompassed by the same pulse so that they will show up as one.*

or a chart because the radar cannot see what is round the next headland. It may not be able to see into harbours either because its view may be blocked by intervening land or other obstructions.

There are four parts to a small boat radar, although these are generally combined into two packages. The transmitter which sends out the radar pulses is usually combined with the rotating antenna. The reflected signals from the land re-enter the antenna and are directed to the receiver, which is usually combined with the display unit. The transmitter sends out very short pulses of energy at very high frequency. The rotating antenna directs these pulses around the horizon and they are reflected back from any solid object which they strike. Immediately after sending out the pulse the antenna is open for reception and the distance of the detected target is measured by the very short time it takes for the radio signal to travel out and back. The return signals from the targets are then processed in the receiver before being displayed in the appropriate position on the display screen.

The radar pulse travels at a rate of 1 mile per 6.2 micro seconds. The radar pulse length is 0.1 micro second on the shorter ranges, which is equivalent to a distance of about 30 metres. On the longer ranges the pulse length is automatically switched to 0.5 microseconds, equivalent to 150 metres (495 feet).

The pulse length determines what the radar shows on the display. If two targets are closer than 150 metres (495 feet) on longer ranges they may be swallowed up in the same pulse and will show up as one target on the display. It is only when you switch to shorter range scales that the position becomes clearer.

The width of the radar beam also affects what is shown on the display. On small boat radars the beam may cover a sector between 2 and 6 degrees wide, depending on the radar. Any targets on the same range coming within this beam will show up as a single target rather than as separate targets. This means that an island may show as part of its associated headland, particularly at longer ranges, but the two should separate as you approach so that the picture becomes clearer. The vertical beam width is much wider, usually about 30 degrees, to allow for the rolling of the boat at sea, but where there is excessive rolling and the beam dips below the horizon, you may temporarily lose the picture over certain sectors. However, this should not normally cause a great deal of concern.

However, radar may also pick up targets such as buoys and boats. It may also pick up returns from the waves which reflect the radar signal. These reflections are known as 'sea clutter' and can create signal saturation for up to a mile around your boat. The return from the sea clutter can be just as strong as those from boats or buoys, so that you may lose these targets when they are close-to, particularly in a rough sea. Radar has a sea clutter adjustment which allows you to turn down the gain in the area around the boat, but of course this cuts down the returns from the solid targets as well as from the sea clutter. Sea clutter is more of a problem in rough sea conditions, and apart from adjusting the sea clutter control to its optimum setting there is not much you can do about it.

Another problem with radar is rain and snow, which also reflect the radar signal. Heavy rain squalls can obliterate large areas of the radar screen, although the returns are less intense than sea clutter and you can often pick out weaker targets by adjusting the gain control. In very heavy rain the problems are similar to those caused by sea clutter.

Small boat radars tend to have a transmitter with around 3kW power output. Although the radar may have a theoretical range of 24 miles there is no guarantee that you will pick up targets at this range. This is because the comparatively low power output will only produce very weak returns even from a strong target at this range. At 24 miles you would only pick up distant mountain tops anyway because the lower targets will be below the horizon. Realistically, you might expect to pick up a cliff coastline ·at, perhaps, 12 miles, large ships and lower coastlines at 8 miles and smaller targets such as yachts and buoys (even when these are fitted with a radar reflector) at possibly no more than 3 miles. These are only rough guidelines and much will depend on the nature of the target, the type of power output of your particular radar and the prevailing conditions. You should try to gain experience using radar in clear weather so that you have sufficient confidence if visibility deteriorates.

Modern, small boat radars are of the daylight viewing type, which means that except in bright sunlight the display does not need to be shielded, making it much easier to view the screen in the wheelhouse of a motor cruiser. Radars with separate control panels give you much more flexibility in the installation, too. This feature allows you to mount the display in the best position for viewing, and the control panel in the best position for operating. The sort of features to look for in a small boat radar are electronic range and bearing markers and signal processing, the latter giving you a much clearer picture with less interference.

Colour radar displays are being introduced into the small boat market; these give a clearer picture, each feature on the display using a different colour. One type of colour radar uses different colours to indicate the various signal strengths but this gives a more confusing rather than a clearer picture and is being replaced by radar which uses monochrome for the targets and alternative colours for features such as range and bearing markers.

Radar Collision Avoidance
Radar is the only piece of electronic equipment which can also be used for collision avoidance. It has a vital role to play in poor visibility, showing you the location of other vessels around you. However, this information should be treated with great caution – considerable experience in the use of radar is required before it can be used for collision avoidance.

The main problem with small boat radars is that they are relative motion radars, which means that your own boat stays firmly in the centre of the screen. The targets representing other vessels move on the display with a combination of their own course and speed as well as the course and speed of your vessel; it is not always easy, therefore, to get a true impression of the movements of other craft. The traditional method of working this out is to carry out a radar plot. This involves plotting the range and bearing of the other targets at regular intervals and then applying your own course and speed to get a true indication of the course and speed of the other vessel. This is a laborious process which is very difficult, if not impossible, to carry out on a

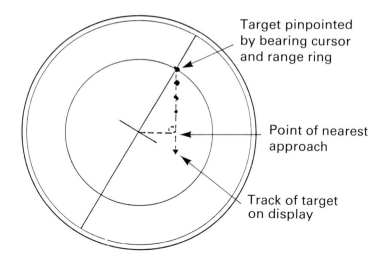

Target pinpointed by bearing cursor and range ring

Point of nearest approach

Track of target on display

Tracking an approaching target on the radar. The first position is fixed by the intersection of the range ring and bearing line. The closest approach is shown by the imaginary line at right angles to the line joining successive target positions. If the bearing does not change a great deal then you are on, or close to, a collision course.

fast motor cruiser, so you need to develop alternative techniques to cope with collision avoidance in poor visibility.

You should try to keep out of the way of other vessels altogether. You can do this on a coastal passage by setting a course inside the bays and close round headlands – areas which are not frequented by larger ships. Similarly, if you are in a buoyed channel, set your course just outside the buoys in the channel, provided there is adequate water, thus leaving the main channel for big ships which need the deeper water. This helps to cut down the number of targets you will have to deal with on the radar screen, but you will still have to cope with other small craft.

The technique here is to set your bearing marker on the target on the radar display as soon as it·is sighted. A target can be 'fixed' on the screen by pinpointing it with the range and bearing markers, then as time goes on you will be able to see where it has progressed in relation to this 'fix'. If the other vessel stays on or close to the bearing marker, then it is heading towards you and there is a risk of collision. If the target moves between the heading marker and the bearing marker then it should pass ahead of you and if it opens out the other side of the heading marker then it should pass astern of you. These are only broad guidelines of course, and any target which stays anywhere near the bearing marker is a threat. If a target comes within one mile you should think about reducing speed and be prepared to stop.

In poor visibility never travel at such a speed that you cannot stop within at least half the range of visibility. This gives you time to take action when you see another craft visually, but if you feel you want to alter course on the radar information alone you must do this in very good time, i.e. when the other craft is still at least a mile away. You should also alter course in a very positive manner to pass well clear. In making such an alteration you should always turn away from rather than towards the target on the screen.

These techniques are fine when you have only one target on the screen to deal with, but when you have two or three targets the position becomes much more complicated and the only real solution is to slow down until you have managed to sort out the situation. You can put the bearing marker on each target in turn to assess their course and speed but remember that they might also be slowing or altering course at the same time as you.

The Log
The log is an important item for motor cruisers, not only to assess the performance of the boat but also as an input for Satnav receivers and for calculating dead reckoning. There are a number of types of log on the market, the main difference between them being the type of impeller used to measure speed.

The traditional towed log used an impeller which was towed through the water on the end of a rope, but this has been largely replaced by a small impeller which is mounted underneath the hull. This can be a paddle-wheel type or a propeller type, the revolutions being counted by a small magnet embedded in the impeller which creates an electronic pulse with each revolution. An alternative is the electro-magnetic log where two electrodes are mounted under the hull and a small induced current is generated between them by the passage of water across them. This current is proportional to the speed. The advantage of this type of log is that there are virtually no projections from the hull, thus reducing the chance of damage from floating debris, but because the log sensor is very close to the hull surface it is not always easy to get a good flow of water across the electrodes.

A new development is the Sonic log, in which a sound signal is sent between two transducers mounted on the hull. The transmission time of the signal varies according to the speed. This type of log is very accurate. The two transducers come mounted in a single bolt-on unit for motor cruiser use. The impeller log can be used at speeds of up to 30 knots, whereas the Sonic log can be used at speeds of up to 40 knots. At higher speeds the only satisfactory type of log tends to be the pitot tube type, which measures the pressure of the water in a tube placed in the water flow. This type of log is used in offshore racing boats and can cope with speeds of up to 80 knots but is very inaccurate at lower speeds.

Apart from the Sonic log, all logs are sensitive to seaweed and are prone to damage from floating debris, both of which can be a problem on fast cruisers. The underwater units are also susceptible to marine growth, which can cause considerable inaccuracies in log readings, particularly with an impeller log. The underwater parts of the log should not be covered with anti-fouling paint and every time the boat is taken out of the water the impellers or transducers should be very carefully cleaned to help the log give consistently reliable results.

On every boat the log needs to be calibrated, and for this you need a measured distance. Marks for this can be found outside some harbours, or you could measure a distance between two marks shown on the chart. You run the boat over the distance in both directions to average out the influences of wind and tide, and from the time taken you can work out the speed. Whilst running over the distance you also take the speed shown on the log; if the measured and the calculated speeds are different the log needs to be adjusted. For this adjustment refer to the log handbook; quite a bit of patience will be required to get the calibration set at different speeds.

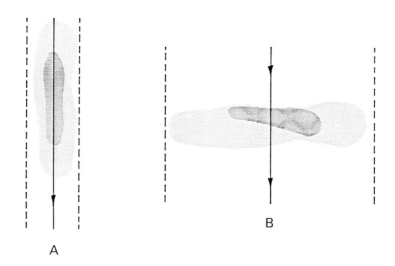

A

B

Soundings can be used to help fix your position. If you pick up the shallow sounding you are somewhere between the dotted lines. In situation A there is a good check on the course made good, but not on the distance. In B the reverse applies.

Echo Sounders

Echo sounders also use underwater transducers so you will need to keep them free from marine growth, too. For the echo sounder to work correctly the transducers should be in solid water. This is not always easy to achieve on a fast planing boat where air bubbles can be introduced into the water passing across the transducer face. On a displacement cruiser the transducer is usually placed just aft of amidships, but on a planing boat it needs to be as far aft as possible to keep it in solid water, although preferably not too close to the propellers, which can cause noise interference. Transom mounting is used on many fast boats.

The echo sounder works by transmitting a sound signal through the water which is reflected from the sea bed. The distance is found by measuring the time between transmission and reception. Like the log, the echo sounder needs to be calibrated to ensure that you are obtaining reliable readings and you can do this at different depths by measuring the depth of the water with a lead line and then checking the echo sounder reading. The echo sounder measures the distance from the transducer face to the sea bed and you may like to correct this to measure the distance from the water surface to the sea bed. Many users prefer to know the depth of water under the boat rather than the actual depth of water itself. Whilst calibration is not so critical in deeper water, it is vital in shallow water – perhaps down to 10 or 20 feet because this is really where you need accurate readings from the echo sounder. When you are working in very shallow water, with only a foot or two under the boat, you may find the echo sounder fails to work. This is because the receiver is closed when the transmitter is working, and the reflected pulse returns before the receiver is open for reception.

There are a variety of different displays available for echo sounders, the most common being that where a light rotates around the display face. This is often a feature of low-cost units. Alternatives are the analogue or digital displays, which now give clear indications of the depth, but if you want historical as well as up-to-date information you will need an echo sounder which shows depths graphically either on a paper chart or a video chart. This type of presentation is useful for navigation and is also the best form of display if your echo sounder doubles up as a fish-finder.

Electronic Compasses

Electronic compasses are growing in popularity. They work on the principle of measuring the earth's magnetic field by means of two sensitive coils which translate the detected magnetic field into electronic signals. These then allow the compass heading to be shown either in analogue or digital form. Electronic compasses are also useful for supplying heading information to a Satnav receiver. They offer much more flexibility in the type of display available compared with a traditional magnetic compass, and it is also possible to build in electronic damping. Fast motor cruisers often have a fairly violent motion and this movement has to be damped out at the compass to obtain steady readings.

Another feature of electronic compasses is the ease with

which they allow you to check deviation. This is done by simply putting the compass into the calibrate mode and turning the boat through 360 degrees. It is important that an absolutely steady rate of turn is achieved, which means that this operation must be carried out in still water conditions with little or no wind. A successful calibration depends upon measuring any fluctuations in the rate of turn shown by the compass compared with the assumed steady rate of turn of the boat. The results of this compass correction should only be used if they show consistency over several successive swings. However, this self-calibration is no substitute for a compass adjuster, who not only finds the errors but also attempts to eliminate them by fitting corrector magnets. Calibration only serves as a check that nothing has changed since the compass adjuster did his job.

When the deviation is found in this way it can be applied automatically to the compass. It is also possible to apply the fixed correction for variation which is applicable to the area in which you operate so that the compass can show the true reading on the display. If you allow these corrections to be applied automatically in this way it might be sensible to put a note to this effect by the side of the compass in case someone else ever uses the boat.

Electronic Charts

Electronic charts are a product of the computer age and although still a comparative rarity on motor cruisers they indicate the way ahead. On fast craft where it is often difficult to use a paper chart they provide a very viable and valuable alternative. Many of the features found on paper charts are displayed on a video screen, and in addition your desired track, as determined by the waypoints you have fed into the position finding equipment, is shown on the chart display, together with the track which you are actually following, so that on one display you have a tactical presentation in real time of the navigation situation. The cross track error can be seen clearly and can also be related to the navigation features which are displayed on the chart, so you have an unambiguous presentation, giving all the information you need for navigating safely at high speed.

Electronic charts come in a variety of forms. Your ability to navigate using only an electronic chart will depend a great deal on the type of display system in use. The most basic form of display is the electronic plotter which simply has a latitude and longitude grid and no actual chart information on the display. This type of presentation is still useful for navigation because your actual and intended tracks are both shown on the display, so that you can relate your actual position to your desired position.

Several plotters on the market can be upgraded by inserting a disc or tape which has the chart information on it, so that this information can then be shown on the display. This chart information tends to be fairly basic, however, usually incorporating only the coast outline and perhaps important buoys and other navigation landmarks. More complex electronic chart presentations allow underwater contour lines, wrecks and other navigation information to be displayed, but even these displays do not show the whole navigation picture and generally have to be used in conjunction with the paper chart.

The difficulty is in presenting the detailed information shown on the paper chart on a comparatively basic video display, which can quickly become overcrowded. To help clarify the picture, navigational information is often presented in layers which can be called up or wiped from the screen at the whim of the navigator, so that there is only the necessary information for one task at a time on the screen. Another problem is that of storing in electronic form the vast amount of information contained on a paper chart. Modern techniques are now overcoming this problem and allow a much more realistic chart presentation.

One of the latest types of electronic chart presentation is almost an exact replica of the paper chart shown on the video display. The chart is digitalised and stored on laser discs; one disc can contain the information covered by a whole series of paper charts. In this way the navigator is presented with a friendly and familiar type of electronic chart display. This is likely to be the way ahead for future developments. The charts are automatically changed on the display as the vessel proceeds along its course. It is also possible to vary the scale of the chart within predetermined limits which relate to the accuracy of the information available on the chart.

A possible future development in this area would be the integration of the radar and the electronic chart onto one screen, which would cut out the land returns from the radar where they coincide with the electronic chart display so that, in effect, only other vessels are shown. However, this is likely to complicate the display to the point where it becomes difficult to interpret. As far as motor cruisers are concerned a more realistic approach in integrating radar and electronic charts would be to present them on adjacent screens, with both working on the same scale and orientated in the same direction. There is no doubt that this type of display will be used more and more on high speed motor cruisers as the price of electronic equipment continues to fall and as users recognise the inadequacies of current navigation systems in terms of safe navigation for fast craft.

Autopilots

Having the boat steered automatically by an autopilot takes a great deal of the boring routine out of passage making and can be particularly valuable if you are short-handed. The autopilot works by taking inputs from a compass and maintaining the vessel on a steady course. This basic principle is followed by all autopilots but there are a great variety of these units on the market today which differ in the degree and variation of their control features to suit different conditions. For instance, it is often possible to limit the amount of rudder used for steering the boat, which prevents the boat swinging about in fine weather, but in rough seas a coarser setting will be required. The same applies to the amount the boat swings before the autopilot starts correcting the swing. In the simpler types of autopilot these limits are set manually, but in the adaptive autopilot the unit senses the movement of the boat and its control through the rudder and compass readings and automatically adapts the autopilot control settings to match the prevailing conditions. These units can also have a built in rudder bias, for instance to compensate for a strong wind that is blowing on the beam.

There are different ways of setting up the autopilot, some requiring you to set the desired course on an analogue dial, and others requiring you to bring the boat onto the desired course and then engage the autopilot. There are also different methods of re-engaging manual steering when you want to override the autopilot (perhaps to avoid another craft or a lobster pot in the water). For instance, you can alter the analogue dial setting to a temporary new course, whilst other systems allow a 10 or 20 degree alteration of course by pressing buttons. Alternatively, there may simply be a disengage button which allows you to take over manual steering immediately. On one of the latest systems, as soon as you turn the wheel of the craft you have manual control. Whichever of these systems you select the important factor is the ease with which you are able to take over manual control. Remember, that you may have to do this in the dark, so the system should be simple.

Interfacing
It is now possible to interface the autopilot with Decca and Loran receivers so that the vessel auomatically follows the desired track to the next waypoint. The position finding receiver can also alter course automatically onto the new track when the waypoint is reached so that you can virtually have automatic steering right from the time you leave harbour till you arrive at your destination. This may be a somewhat daunting prospect to many boat owners and it is a step down the route towards automation which many may be reluctant to follow. However, there is no denying the value of an autopilot in that it allows you to concentrate on navigation or other jobs around the boat, but you must be aware of the need to keep a proper look-out at all times, not just for other craft but also for floating debris which could cause damage to your boat. The course steered by the autopilot should be checked at regular intervals to make sure that it is obeying instructions. Some autopilots are fitted with an off-course alarm to give warning of any deviations. The autopilot itself actuates an electric or hydraulic motor which in turn drives the steering. The maintenance of this interface machinery should be carried out as detailed in the handbook to ensure reliable operation.

COMMUNICATIONS

VHF Radio

The ability to communicate with the shore and with other vessels is now almost vital for motor cruisers, and you are spoilt for choice in the methods available. The choice of communication system will depend a great deal on where and how you operate your boat. However, a marine VHF radio is now almost essential for any boat. Radios which work on the VHF band are cheap and easy to install and provide reliable communications over approximately a 20 mile range. In most areas this enables you to maintain constant communication with the coastguard and also provides a link with marinas and harbour authorities which are radio equipped. VHF radio is also the normal link for talking to other boats although boat-to-boat the range may be reduced to 10 miles. The range you will get with a VHF radio will depend on the antenna height of both the transmitting and receiving stations because the radio links only operate when the antennae can 'see' each other.

Modern VHF radios are generally very simple to operate. Channel 16 is the primary distress and calling channel; you then switch to working frequencies as appropriate. Channel selection is done simply by setting the appropriate number on the control panel keyboard.

Single Sideband Radio

For a greater range of reliable radio communications an SSB radio is necessary. This can operate on medium frequencies, with 2182 kcs being the primary distress and calling frequency. Alternatively, there are more expensive radios which encompass both medium (MF) and high (HF) frequency. MF radio will operate on ranges up to around 200 miles, whereas HF radio has a range suitable for transmitting from mid-ocean to the shore. An HF radio is probably only justified on a motor cruiser if you travel extensively and want to make radio links back to your home country. Otherwise an MF radio, which has lower power requirements, will be sufficient (even when you are some distance from the shore) and will also provide a reliable means of initiating distress signals. Both MF and HF radios require long antennae, perhaps up to 9 metres, and the power drain when transmitting can be very high.

CB Radios and Cellular Telephones

VHF, MF and HF radios are all specifically designed for marine use, but it is also possible to use equipment such as CB radio and cellular telephones at sea. The latter, in particular, can be a very effective means of communication because it provides direct dialling access to the shore telephone system; similarly, calls can be received on board direct from shore telephones. Coverage of cellular telephone systems varies from country to country and a system operating in one country is unlikely to be compatible with another. This situation is likely to change and eventually there may be a fully compatible European cellular telephone system.

One advantage of cellular telephones is that they can be used when you are in harbour. If you have a portable unit you can transfer it from your boat to your car, office or home as required. CB radios offer the same type of benefits but you do have to know who you are calling at the other end. In the USA the Coast Guard maintains a listening watch on some CB channels but at present it is the only country with this facility.

Emergency Radio

Cellular telephones and CB radios are not a substitute for marine band radios because they have no facility to cope with emergency requirements. As a minimum you should have a VHF marine radio on board to cope with emergencies. This, possibly combined with a cellular telephone, will provide you with all the communication facilities you need, provided you stay within reasonable range of the shore.

Whilst radio is a vital means of communication in an emergency an EPIRB (Emergency Position Indicating Radio Beacon) can be a simple way of alerting people if you are in distress. These fully waterproof independent radio units transmit a distress alert call on aircraft distress frequencies which are also monitored by satellite so that, as well as indicating distress, your position can be pinpointed. The biggest problem with an EPIRB is that you cannot indicate to the rescue services the *type* of distress you are in.

EPIRBs can provide a useful additional alerting method in case your electrical system on board fails. Otherwise the VHF or MF radio is the logical way to indicate distress. MF and HF radios are fitted with an automatic distress signal which allows anyone hearing it to take a bearing of your position even if you are unable to transmit a normal voice distress call. The main benefit of using radio for a distress call is that you will know that someone has received the call and is acting on it. You can also explain your specific problems so that the correct help can be sent.

A crowded dashboard where the electronics for navigation have been added as an afterthought. The compass located between the rev counters may not give reliable information.

Satellite Communications

In the future, satellite communications may become viable for motor cruiser use. The Standard-C terminal developed by Inmarsat will provide telex links both to and from the boat without the need for the large dish aerial normally associated with satellite communications. For those needing a reliable means of keeping in touch with home or business, this terminal could provide a useful link outside the normal range of VHF or MF radio. Satellite communications are usually completely free from interference, and much more reliable than other radio links. You have to pay for this better quality reception in terms of a much higher cost, although this may change in the future. There are also telex facilities associated with normal marine radio systems.

Another form of telex service, in the receive only mode, is Navtex, which is a small single-channel telex receiver used for receiving distress, navigation warnings and weather forecasts. The whole operation is totally automatic and as the messages are printed out or displayed on a video screen there is no excuse for not keeping abreast of such vital safety information.

INSTALLATION

The installation of electronic equipment on board a motor cruiser is something that many designers and builders ignore, so that when an owner decides to fit the equipment, it often has to be mounted in a position which is not always the best for easy use. This is an aspect of motor cruiser design that will eventually change but at present if you want to install equipment you have to make use of whatever space is available. It can often be difficult to find suitable space for a radar without blocking the view through the windscreen and this is even more difficult when the control panel is incorporated, so that it has to be mounted within easy reach of the steering position. The installation often ends up as something of a compromise and it pays to spend time in careful design and planning to optimise the positions of electronic equipment as far as possible because you will probably use this equipment more than any other when you are at sea.

Display screens should be positioned where they are not subject to glare or reflections, control panels should be easily accessible and the night-time lighting of instruments and its effect on your night vision should be carefully considered. The effects of electronic equipment on your steering compass should also be considered; items such as radar usually have a safe compass distance marked on the display unit which should be respected.

With so much electronic equipment now being installed in motor cruisers the problem of finding a suitable location for all the required antennae can be quite difficult. Priority should be given to the VHF radio antenna which requires as much height as possible and therefore should be at the masthead to give the greatest effective range. In general, the radar scanner needs to be as high as possible too and the normal position for this is either on the wheelhouse top or, if the boat is fitted with an arch mast, on the centre line of this mast. The antennae required for Decca and Loran should be sited as far away as possible from transmitting antennae, particularly for MF or HF radio. Both Decca and Loran are very sensitive to electrical and electronic interference and so the antennae should be placed as far as possible from the engine compartment and other sources of electrical noise.

Much will depend on the layout of your boat, but one way of testing a position is to make a temporary installation and then check the signal/noise level shown on the instrument when you have the engine running at both slow and full speed. Then try moving the antennae to a different position and see whether there is any improvement in the signal/noise level. The handbook will indicate what is an acceptable signal/noise level, but the higher this figure the better, and it is worth spending a little time to try to get the optimum arrangement.

Both Decca and Loran also require efficient grounding; this should involve a separate wire direct to a propeller shaft bracket or stern drive leg. Alternatively, you could install a dedicated earthing plate on the bottom of the boat for grounding electronic equipment.

Power supplies to electronic equipment are also an important consideration because electronics do not function well if there are wild fluctuations in power supply. If you have an MF or HF radio on board, therefore, these should not be supplied from the same battery as the other electronic equipment because the high power requirements of the radios tend to create surges in the electrical circuits. Each piece of equipment should be individually fused. In many instances the manufacturers incorporate a fuse into the equipment, but this is often located inside the receiver so that if a fuse blows at sea it involves a dismantling job in far from ideal surroundings. For this reason try to select electronic equipment with an easily accessible outside fuse.

Essential electronic equipment such as the position finding equipment and possibly the echo sounder should be wired so that it is possible to switch rapidly over to an alternative power supply if the main supply fails. You could also incorporate the navigation lights and the VHF radio into this emergency circuit,

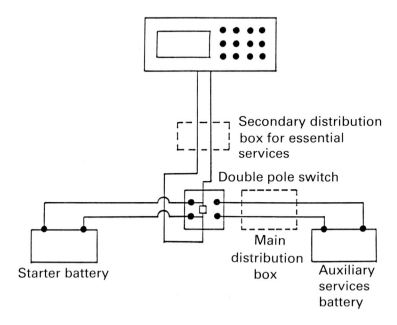

How to rig an alternative power supply from the starter battery for electronic position finding equipment. The double pole switch allows the alternative battery to supply the essential services.

and by using a double-pole switch the alternative power supply could quickly be brought into use in the event of a power failure.

RULES AND REGULATIONS

The only rules and regulations which cover the use of electronics on board concern transmitters. Apart from the obvious ones like radios, the transmitters you have on board will include the EPIRB and radar, and in many countries you are required to have a licence for them. This involves having the vessel inspected to ensure that the installation conforms with the requirements; you are then issued with a certificate to display. If you only have a VHF radio obtaining a licence is only a formality but it is still necessary to take an examination in order to conform with the law (see below).

If you have any radio transmitter on board you are required to have an individual licence to operate the radio. This is largely designed to prevent misuse of this vital piece of safety equipment. Before you can obtain a licence you must take a short examination to ensure that you understand the correct radio procedures for both routine and emergency operation. The examination is quite simple and straightforward. It is possible to attend a short course to familiarise yourself with the necessary procedures; this is an essential prerequisite of having a radio on board; it is a small price to pay for the valuable benefits, in terms of convenience and peace of mind.

9 · Wheelhouse and Accommodation

The design of every motor cruiser is something of a compromise and this is nowhere more apparent than in the wheelhouse and accommodation. The designer has to match the conflicting requirements of using the boat efficiently at sea and providing a comfortable environment when living aboard in harbour. It is not impossible to match up these often conflicting requirements as many of the good designs on the market demonstrate. However, the owner of a motor cruiser should appreciate where the compromises have been made so that he can get the best out of the boat. There is a strong tendency to switch the emphasis towards use of the boat in harbour, but there is a great deal that an owner can do to redress the balance to suit his particular needs.

In harbour an owner will expect his boat to provide a reasonably stable platform and also many of the comforts and conveniences found at home. Used in this way the boat is, in effect, a country cottage or mobile home. Out at sea, however, the environment changes. You should expect a reasonable degree of comfort, even out at sea, but not to the extent that it impinges on the efficient operation of the boat whilst underway. The ultimate in sea-going efficiency is found in craft such as pilot boats and lifeboats which have a very difficult job to do in uncompromising conditions at sea. Motor cruisers do not need to go to these lengths but as an owner you should appreciate the requirements for operating a boat at sea.

MOVING ABOUT IN THE BOAT

Life on board becomes much more comfortable both at sea and in harbour if you can move about the boat easily. In harbour one of the more difficult aspects of motor cruising is actually getting on board the boat. As the freeboard (the distance between the waterline and the deck) of motor cruisers has tended to increase in order to give more space below decks, and at the same time marina pontoons have become lower, there is a considerable gap to bridge when climbing aboard. One motor cruiser design incorporates a step in the hull to facilitate climbing on board in harbour. The alternative is to have a single or double step on the pontoon, but this should be secured in place. There should be something to grab hold of when climbing aboard, and a strategically placed handhold for this purpose will be welcomed by your guests, as will a small step inside the cockpit at the boarding point. This can bridge the large vertical gap between the deck level and the cockpit floor, which gives you a chance to step on board with a degree of dignity!

With Mediterranean mooring where the boat is stern to the

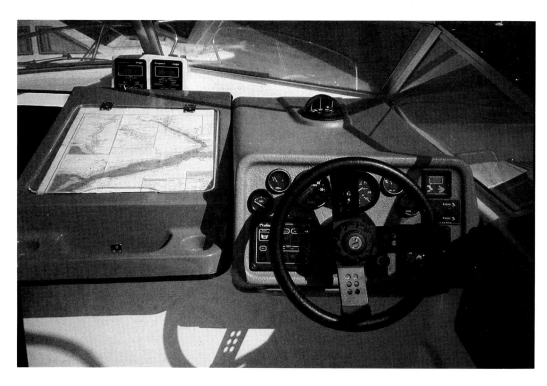

The provision of a flat surface near the steering position to display a chart is a useful feature.

quay a stern gangway is used for access to the boat. Each boat and mooring will present its own problems but since motor cruisers are increasingly becoming a centre of social activity you should consider the problem of access carefully because it can make life very much more comfortable for everyone.

Once on board, moving about from the cockpit into the saloon is usually fairly easy because full-height doors are now commonplace. Going down below into the accommodation, using short, often narrow ladders, can be more difficult, and here again strategically placed handholds can be useful both in harbour and at sea. Within the confines of the accommodation it is a good idea to cover any sharp corners or edges with padding in order to avoid accidental injury.

Handholds are essential to maintain your balance when moving around the boat, especially when out at sea. If you have nothing to hold on to you run the risk of being thrown about the boat, with the possibility of injury. This is often one of the areas where boat builders economise, but you can improve the situation by fitting handholds in strategic places. It is sometimes difficult to establish the best positions for the handholds; only experience at sea will demonstrate the correct positions. A compromise will often be necessary because a well-placed handhold at sea may hamper movement about the boat when in harbour. Remember, too, that handholds should be quite strong because you often need to put your full weight on them if the boat lurches unexpectedly.

Carpets, fitted to give an air of luxury, are fine in harbour but are not always practical out at sea. If you have carpets they should certainly be fastened down to prevent them slipping. Alternatively, take up the carpets when you go to sea and have a non-slip deck covering underneath – a much more practical surface in sea conditions. This approach also prevents the carpets being damaged by sea water and is a practical way of changing the interior of the boat to meet the needs of both sea and harbour.

SEATING

Comfortable seating is needed on board for use both in harbour and at sea. Standing up for long periods can be very tiring, especially when you are bracing yourself against the movement of the boat and holding on tightly. You need only relax your guard for a moment and you can suddenly find that the boat has lurched unexpectedly, throwing you across the wheelhouse. Whilst it is possible to stand up for short periods at sea, indeed it can be quite enjoyable to do this, particularly on a fast boat, there should be a seat on board for every member of the crew. Converting the comfortable saloon seats that you have in harbour into useful sea-going seats requires a degree of ingenuity. Usually, seats are provided for the helmsman and one other crew member in the forepart of the wheelhouse or cockpit but the rest of the crew tend to be left to their own devices.

The helmsman's seat is often provided with a footrest, enabling you to brace yourself against the movement of the boat;

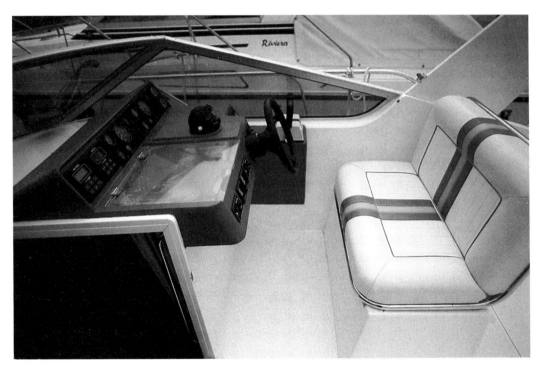

A typical sports cruiser steering position where the seating does not give adequate support and the dash layout can be confusing.

in this way you have both hands free to control the boat. On larger motor cruisers the helmsman's seat may be one half of a double seat. This is not always a good idea because having someone sitting alongside you when you are driving can interfere with the free movement of the steering wheel. Unless your companion in the double seat is provided with suitable handholds he may slide into you when the boat is rolling, preventing you from driving properly.

In a displacement boat the control position is not quite so critical because things happen at a slower pace, but in a planing boat the location of the controls and the layout of the driving area are much more critical. Although there is not a great deal you can do to change this aspect of the boat's design, you can adapt the steering position so that you have a comfortable seat to brace yourself against the movement of the boat. Getting the footrest adjustment and the seat position just right can help a great deal.

It is equally important for the rest of the crew to be seated comfortably. Ideally, they should all be able to see outside from their seats because this helps reduce the risk of seasickness and disorientation. This is not always practical, however, and some of the crew may have to make do with the saloon settee or the bench seats in the cockpit. There are often few handholds here, and on a planing boat life can become quite miserable for them, taking much of the pleasure out of the passage. Much can be done to alleviate the situation by fitting seatbelts. A simple lap strap would be adequate for the purpose but it is much more comfortable to have a full harness with shoulder straps as well as a lap strap so that they can relax completely in the knowledge that the seatbelt will keep them secure. Lifeboat crews now use seatbelts, and whilst you are not likely to meet these sort of extreme conditions, seatbelts can help a great deal to increase comfort on board at sea. This applies not only to the crew sitting on the saloon settees but also to those having the benefit of the forward facing wheelhouse seats. Seatbelts do not have to meet the rigorous strength requirements for cars, so they can simply be bolted through adjacent wood or GRP structures and tucked away out of sight in harbour.

BERTHS

There has been a tendency amongst boat designers to fit as many berths into a boat as possible, because this was once the yardstick by which boat size was judged. Squeezing berths into a boat irrespective of the other facilities provided on board is a somewhat negative approach to boat design. Fortunately, this trend is now changing and comfortable facilities for living on board are now the order of the day. If berths for four people are provided there should be adequate seating in the wheelhouse for the same number of people (and perhaps a couple of extra guests). The galley and toilet facilities should also be adequate for the same numbers.

The trend now is towards introducing a great deal of comfort on board so that most of the facilities of home are provided, including the provision of large double berths, at least in the owner's cabin, and full length berths throughout the vessel so that everyone can sleep in a reasonable degree of comfort. This trend is fine for harbour use, but if you plan to use your sleeping accommodation out at sea it needs more critical consideration. What provides a good night's sleep in harbour is not always the best solution at sea when the boat is moving about.

At sea you want a berth which will stop you being thrown out. There is no easy way to achieve this without major modifications, and you may have to accept this fact and learn to live with it. The chances are that you will not spend a lot of time sleeping at sea anyway, certainly not as much time as you will spend sleeping in harbour.

THE GALLEY

The galley on a motor cruiser represents quite a challenge to the designer. Meals may be produced quickly and easily in harbour but the galley also has to provide a safe stowage for all the equipment used for food preparation. Ideally, it should also be usable at sea in fine conditions. It is the movement of the boat which makes it difficult to cook at sea (or even just heating water). Indeed, boats often move in a way which makes it positively dangerous to cook at sea. Hot liquids and fast boats certainly do not go together. However, you will spend comparatively little time at sea running at speed so the absence of hot food should not be a particular problem.

On slower boats the motion is usually less marked and there may well be a chance of doing some cooking. To facilitate this the galley stove must be fitted with rails (fiddles) so that you can secure the pots and pans to the stove. These can be useful even in harbour because you always have to bear in mind that the wash of a passing boat could make the boat jump around, which could be enough to make the pots slide off the stove. The boat movement is something you should always be aware of when cooking; the risk of accidents involving hot liquids is always present, particularly when you are working in such a confined space.

Cooking Fuels

There is a variety of galley stoves on the market but the type which uses bottled gas fuel is probably the most popular. It is certainly the most convenient – although within the confines of a motor cruiser you need to take care with a bottled gas installation. First, the bottles themselves should be stowed in a separate locker outside in the cockpit or on deck; this locker should have drain holes in the bottom so that any gas which might leak, being heavier than air, will drain out overboard. The pipework for the system should be very carefully installed to minimise the chance of leaks. During the boat's annual overhaul it is a sensible precaution to brush over all the pipework joints in the system with soapy water to check for leaks; leaks will be obvious by the bubbles which appear in the soap. Flexible sections of piping in particular should be thoroughly checked, as well as the stove itself.

The main danger from gas leaks in a bottled gas system arises from the fact that gas is heavier than air. Leaking gas will collect in the bilges of the boat where it can form an explosive mixture. Every year there are accidents caused by this mixture exploding, and a gas detection system with sensors in the bilges – particularly in the engine compartment – is a must if you have bottled gas on board. It only takes a spark to set off the mixture, a spark which could come from any electrical switch or even the starter motor when you turn the engine key.

Bottled gas is also used for water heating and for powering refrigerators on some boats. The convenience of using one fuel for all these functions is obvious. Gas is clean and convenient but one of the products of gas combustion is water, so condensation problems are common. An appliance which uses a lot of gas, such as a water heater, needs an outside ventilating flue. The other point to bear in mind when using gas for any purpose on board is that it needs a good supply of fresh air to burn, so the boat must not be closed up completely when gas is in use.

Other fuels which can be used in the galley stove are alcohol, paraffin (kerosene) and (on larger motor cruisers) even electric cookers. Alcohol and kerosene are less convenient for cooking because they do not light immediately, are difficult to store and are generally less efficient that bottled gas. Cooking with electricity is increasingly more popular. If you only want to cook in harbour you can tie up to a marina berth where a supply is available and plug straight into the mains. The alternative is to have a generator on board. This is now a possibility on motor cruisers over 30 feet (9 metres) in length. There is no doubt that cooking by electricity offers convenience and cleanliness. It also offers the possibility of using a microwave oven, which uses less power than an ordinary cooker and offers a very safe and effective means of cooking even when the boat is moving. Microwave ovens which operate on 12 or 24 volt DC systems are becoming available and may be the solution to many motor cruiser cooking requirements.

Refrigerators are now common on boats and can operate on gas or electricity. In some cases they can operate on both, so that electricity is used when the engine is running but gas is used in harbour to save too great a drain on the battery. Some fridges will even operate on mains power as well, so that you can plug into the shore circuits when in harbour. Whilst the fridge operates in exactly the same way as a domestic fridge in your home, remember that when the boat is bouncing around at sea so are all the contents of the fridge! Careful stowage and the use of sealed containers is a must if you don't relish the unwelcome sight of a mixture of foods when you open the fridge door after a passage,

Stowage

The same goes for storing food in lockers. Sealed plastic containers are the only practical way to store food on board. Stowage of food and equipment in the galley needs a lot of thought. Plates, pots and pans, and cutlery must all be stored securely when you go to sea — even if you have modern, unbreakable plastic crockery, it can still rattle around and make an unpleasant noise in the galley every time you hit a wave.

As it is difficult to use the galley at sea, an option worth considering if you simply want to make hot drinks is a small electric kettle or boiler. These can work off the battery supply and although they use a lot of current this should not present a problem as long as the kettle is used only when the engines are running. The fact that the water is contained inside the kettle when it is being heated up introduces a measure of safety, but you still have to be extremely careful when pouring the water. Both the kettle and the cups should be securely stowed so that only minimum handling is necessary. You can then keep one hand free to hold on with.

THE TOILET

Toilets are one area where designers show considerable ingenuity in squeezing a great deal into a very small space. In the average boat toilet compartment there is barely room to turn round, but within this space there is often a toilet, shower and wash basin. In some installations, however, you have to be something of a contortionist to use the facilities!

The most common type of marine toilet has water in the bowl permanently. On a boat which is bouncing around at sea this is not really acceptable because the water usually ends up everywhere. An alternative is the vacuum toilet, which uses only the minimum of water for flushing and does not spill over when the boat is moving around in waves. Many port and harbour authorities are now demanding the use of enclosed toilet systems which do not deposit sewage directly into the sea, so vacuum toilets are likely to be used increasingly on boats.

On a boat which is moving around, it is important to have something to hold on to in the toilet compartment. Boat builders rarely include handholds, so it is up to you to provide them. Experimentation will soon show you the obvious places where the handholds are needed. Stowage of items in the toilet compartment also requires some thought before you go to sea; the same tactics as those used in the galley are appropriate.

The toilet compartment probably accounts for more water inlet and outlet pipes passing through the hull than any other area. On all these pipes the seacocks should be turned off before you go to sea. If sea water is used for flushing the toilet and it has an overboard outlet you will need to open and close the seacocks each time you want to use the toilet. This can be a considerable inconvenience but it is worth it from the safety point of view.

HEATING

Cruiser owners these days like to have all the comforts of home on their boats. There is a wide variety of equipment available to provide these comforts. For example, if you use your boat in temperate climates you can often greatly extend the cruising season by installing a heating system. Even though you may not want to cruise in the winter, if you have heating on board you can use your boat in harbour as a second home or as an escape from the city. If you only want to use the heating system when you are in harbour and there is a shore power supply available then you may consider installing electric heating, perhaps in the form of fan heaters. These are clean and convenient and will not cause condensation.

If you need heating out at sea as well as in harbour there are a variety of systems to choose from, but diesel and bottled gas are the most common. Since diesel is used in the engine it may be advantageous to use it in the heating system too. Modern diesel heaters are clean and efficient and are usually associated with a ducted hot air system that provides a form of central heating for the boat. It is possible to have the heating system linked to a hot water heating system so that in one unit you serve all of the boat's heating requirements. It is important to remember that both diesel and bottled gas heating systems require a separate flue to take fumes away from the boat. The operation of a heating and hot water system should be trouble free, although some

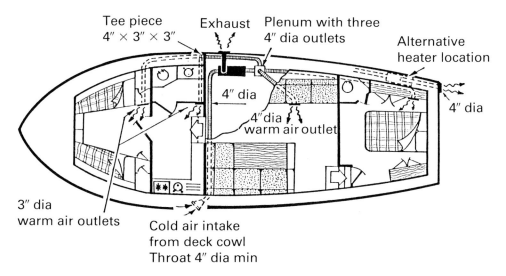

A central heating system for a motor cruiser greatly extends the cruising season in colder climates. In hot climates air conditioning could replace the heater if you have adequate power supplies.

maintenance will be required – an annual check should be sufficient.

Whilst a central heating system offers the ultimate in luxury in colder weather, a cheaper form of heating can be provided by individual bottled gas heaters. A catalytic type of heater which has no exposed flame is probably safer for use on a boat but since there will be no outside ventilation water from the combustion process is likely to cause condensation.

VENTILATION

Because the fumes from heaters are not always vented outside you will need adequate ventilation on your boat, both to ensure a fresh supply of air for burning the fuel and to help remove exhaust gases. Ventilation is just as important as heating; in the hot summer months it can help make life on board more pleasant. Doors, hatches and opening ports all contribute to ventilation and are fine for use in hot sunny weather. Remember, though, that you will also need ventilation when it is pouring with rain (when you won't want to open hatches and doors). You may also want ventilation at sea when the boat has to be battened down to prevent spray coming in. Even when the boat is left locked up in harbour some form of ventilation will keep the boat fresh and prevent condensation (which may damage fabrics and furnishings). There are a wide variety of ventilators on the market which allow air to circulate but which keep the water out. Boat builders usually build in vents over the galley and toilet compartments but additional vents can also be fitted in the deckhead of the cabin to increase the circulation of air when the boat is closed up.

Most of the time you will be using your motor cruiser in fine weather and if your boat has an enclosed wheelhouse it can be very frustrating having to stay inside when it is bright and sunny outside. Having a fly-bridge is an obvious solution to this dilemma, and the sports cruiser is another. Windows which open fully and a sunshine roof in the wheelhouse can go a long way to making life more pleasant if you have an enclosed wheelhouse. Wheelhouse windows which open fully can prove difficult to keep watertight when conditions are not so pleasant, however. Designers *are* getting better at solving these problems, but getting the heating and ventilation just right on a motor cruiser requires a lot of experimentation and adjustment. If you are going to be in hot climates for any length of time it is a good idea to have air conditioning. This has the disadvantage of using up a great deal of power, and can only be operated satisfactorily if you have either a shore power supply or generators which can provide sufficient power on board.

LIGHTING

Nights spent aboard a motor cruiser can be made much more pleasant if you have a good lighting system. Fluorescent lights are economical on battery power and provide good, if harsh, lighting. They can also generate considerable electrical interference which may upset radios and other electronic equipment, particularly at sea. A combination of fluorescent and conventional electric light bulbs is the best answer overall.

Lighting in the wheelhouse should be carefully considered because different sorts of lighting will be required in different conditions. For example, bright lighting may be required in harbour but at sea this, together with light coming from the instruments, may cause reflections in the wheelhouse windows. Bright lights may also affect night vision. It is a good idea to use red lights in the wheelhouse at night. You should also use a red light at the chart table to reduce glare.

THE WHEELHOUSE

You will spend a great deal of your time at sea in the wheelhouse and there is scope here for making changes which can not only make life more comfortable but also achieve a better interface between you and the boat. It is particularly important that the seating at the steering position is right because you may spend long hours here and comfort is important if you are to remain efficiently in control of the boat. Seats are rarely adjustable in anything but the fore and aft direction. If necessary, insert blocks to raise the seat or adjust its angle to suit your requirements.

If the design of the boat is good, both the steering wheel and the throttle should come nicely to hand and be easy to use, but this is rarely the case. You may be able to vary the angle of the steering wheel housing and you can also make certain adjustments to the throttles in the same way. An angled steering wheel can often be more comfortable than a vertical wheel — which is the normal fitment. Since you will be using the ahead part of the throttles practically all the time this should be located in the most comfortable position. If you do adjust the throttle box, make sure you don't compromise the astern movement. If you have to use the throttles a great deal at sea when driving the boat through waves a strategically placed arm rest close to the throttle box can greatly minimise the fatigue, but make sure that it does not interfere with the free movement of the throttles.

The wheelhouse steering position is the focus of a motor cruiser. Just as in a car, this area should receive a lot of attention. However, don't ignore the comfort of your passengers and crew by concentrating on the steering position alone. You go motor cruising for pleasure and everybody on board should be able to derive pleasure from running the boat at sea as well as being comfortable in harbour. So the wheelhouse, deck saloon or steering position, whichever is the appropriate name for the particular way your boat is laid out, should be thought out carefully. Designers tend to place the emphasis on comfortable living in harbour and it is left to you to develop it for comfortable use at sea.

STOWAGE

Anything that can move about on a motor cruiser is a liability. This applies to the crew as well as the equipment. Seatbelts are a good idea for the crew to locate themselves when the boat is at sea. As far as equipment is concerned, you should make sure that everything is secured in place. Boat builders are generally very bad about providing suitable stowage space. Lockers and drawers in which you can stow equipment are all very well, but there are many things which you need to secure *inside* the lockers, and you will probably have to provide the means of doing this yourself.

The heavy items are the ones you need to worry about. For example, anchors, spare propellers and drums of oil should all be properly secured. Any slight movement will start wear and tear, may cause damage and can eventually lead to the item breaking free from its stowage. The only way to secure these items is to bolt them in place. The anchor may be stowed on the bow in the bow roller, in which case it should be very firmly secured. *If* it is stowed in a locker there should be some means of clamping it in place. Rope lashings are not adequate for this purpose because the anchor will eventually work itself loose. The only real solution is to make special clamps to hold the anchor absolutely securely. The same goes for spare propellers – indeed, any other heavy items of equipment. For lighter items, rubber cord is ideal because it stays tight and is useful for holding irregularly shaped objects. You can use it to stow equipment at the steering position, such as binoculars, dividers and parallel rules. It can be equally useful for stowing plates and other items in the galley.

You should be systematic about stowage; everything should have its place and should be in that place when you go to sea. You will thus have no difficulty in finding things when you want them and they will also be in good condition and ready for use. The way in which equipment is stowed on board can make the difference between a well-run motor cruiser and a chaotic (and potentially hazardous) one.

If you carry an outboard motor the logical way to stow this is by using the transom clamp, making up a substitute bracket for the motor to be stowed on. A good place to stow a petrol motor is on the rail at the stern to prevent leakages and fumes down below, but if you must stow the motor below it should be kept upright. You could fix a similar clamp in the engine compartment, but be very careful about petrol fumes leaking into the bilges. Fuel for the outboard should be somewhere up on deck so that it can easily be dumped if there is a fire on board but equally so that there is no risk of fumes finding their way below. The best position for this fuel is underneath the cockpit seats or in deck lockers. If you have an inflatable dinghy which you keep folded up and stowed below in a locker make sure there are no sharp edges on which the dinghy can chafe if it moves around; much more harm is done to inflatable dinghies when they are stowed than when they are being used.

Glass bottles for alcoholic drinks are probably one of the most difficult items to stow, along with glasses (which are always more pleasant to drink from than plastic beakers). This is one area where boat builders usually score well by providing proper stowage, although you can always improve on this with the use of plastic cord or foam because the stowages are rarely tight enough to prevent movement altogether. It would be a tragedy, having just arrived in harbour, to open the drinks cabinet and find broken glasses and bottles just at the time when you want a celebratory drink.

The engine compartment and the space around the steering gear are two areas where particular attention should be paid to stowage. In both these areas there are moving control rods and levers, so nothing must be allowed to move around which could interfere with their free operation. Many owners take great risks with their steering gear by stowing buckets, fenders and other equipment in this area, which could cause the steering to jam at an inopportune moment and perhaps bring your boating career to an abrupt end.

10 · Engines and propulsion

The engines are perhaps the most vital part of a motor cruiser because if you lose the power of your engines you lose control. There is a long tradition amongst yachtsmen not to rely 100 per cent on anything, and for years motor cruisers carried auxiliary sails. Those days have passed, however, and a modern motor cruiser puts total faith in its engines. This faith is justified partly because a large number of modern boats have twin engine installations and partly because modern engines are extremely reliable anyway. The vulnerability of modern engines lies in the systems which support them, i.e. the fuel system, the electrical system, the cooling system and the exhaust system.

Marine engines are produced in large numbers and manufacturers spend a lot of time and money testing and developing them to ensure reliability. By contrast, boats are built in tens, or at best in hundreds, so there are not the same resources for evaluation and testing, which means that the engine installation is largely dependent on experience rather than based on thorough testing. The result of this is that the installation of the support systems for the engines is rarely of the same high standard as the manufacture of the engines. However, as an owner you can do a great deal to improve the situation and to ensure that the support systems are maintained to a high standard.

ENGINE TYPES

There are two main types of engine; those which run on petrol (gasoline) and those which run on diesel. Arguments rage about the relative merits of each, but in reality the gap between them is narrowing to the point where the cost of the fuel could well be the deciding factor in your choice of engine. Boat builders often offer a choice between petrol and diesel installations but it is not always easy for the prospective buyer to make an informed decision. The main factors to consider are cost, safety, performance and reliability.

Engine Costs
In general, a petrol engine will be cheaper than a diesel engine, and this can be an influencing factor. In considering cost you also have to look at the cost of the fuel – in general diesel fuel is cheaper than petrol. However, when you consider the average use of a motor cruiser throughout a season, the difference in cost between these two fuels is not likely to be great and probably

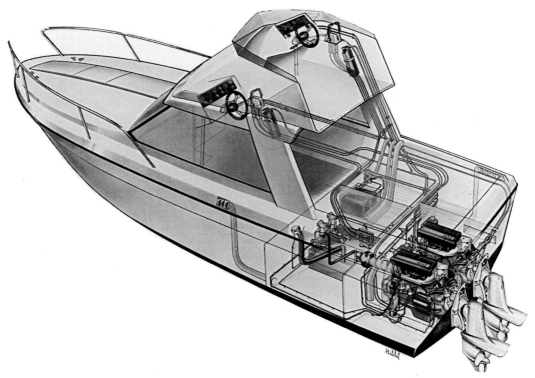

The layout of the engine and steering systems on a typical twin-engined stern drive motor cruiser. (Photo: Volvo Penta)

will not greatly influence the way you use your boat, whereas the purchase price of the boat could be more important to you.

Safety
The comparative volatility of diesel and petrol is the main factor to be considered as far as safety is concerned. Petrol ignites and/or explodes much more readily than diesel although this does not necessarily make its use more dangerous in a motor cruiser. The risks are not significantly greater provided you have a well engineered fuel system. The risks with petrol generally arise from a badly maintained fuel system where leaks may occur, allowing petrol to seep into the bilges where it can form an explosive mixture. The sensor used to detect gas leakage can also detect dangerous levels of petrol vapour in the bilges. Exhaust fans can also remove any fumes which might gather in the bilges and are a mandatory fitting on petrol engine installations, to be used before the engine is started so that the sparks from the starter motor do not ignite any vapour mixture in the bilges. There are inherent dangers with petrol installations and one hears horror stories of boats exploding, particularly after refuelling, so if you have a petrol installation you must accept that ongoing maintenance and inspection are necessary to maintain high standards.

   With an engine that runs on diesel fuel the risks in this respect are reduced, but you must be equally disciplined in your approach to using this fuel because diesel engines, with their very fine tolerances, are much more sensitive to dirt and water in the fuel. A properly engineered fuel system should not present any difficulties, as long as you carry out regular maintenance checks.

Reliability
In terms of reliability, petrol engines have a reputation for being second best, largely because of the ignition system; because a high voltage is needed, the ignition does not always take kindly to the damp marine environment. However, in recent years great advances have been made in waterproofing engine electrical systems and in raising standards to improve reliability. If you compare the diesel engine's susceptibility to dirt and water in

the fuel to the vulnerability of petrol engines to damp conditions there is probably little to choose between them in terms of reliability.

Performance

In displacement motor cruisers the type of engine you have does not have much bearing on performance because weight is not critical. In a planing motor cruiser, however, the power/weight ratio of the engine has a considerable influence on performance. Petrol engines are always lighter than diesel engines of a comparable horsepower — so if performance is your hardstick then the petrol engine will probably be your choice. However, diesel engines have improved immeasurably in recent years and

Twin powerful petrol engines on a sports cruiser. Note the quality and spaciousness of the installation, which makes maintenance easy.

it is now possible to get close to petrol engine performance from a diesel engine.

Another, more subtle, aspect to consider in your choice of engine is acceleration. Petrol engines will always give you better

A twin outboard sports cruiser. The outboards have to be bolted on for security but can be removed for servicing or during lay-up.

acceleration and a faster response to the throttles; this can be important in a fast, lightweight sports cruiser in which a good engine response is required to drive the boat in waves. The more ponderous diesel takes a little longer to respond to the throttles, which you may find unacceptable if performance rather than comfort is your main concern.

In general, then, if you have a motor cruiser running up to speeds of 30–35 knots the reassuring thud of a diesel engine will probably be the best choice. If you are looking for performance above this mark the petrol engine will come out on top. This is by no means a hard and fast rule, however – some of the fastest racing boats on the offshore scene today use diesel engines. The important aspect in making your choice of engine is to get a happy combination. Rather than considering the boat or the engine in isolation, remember that they have to work together as a team. It is important to have units which are comfortably compatible.

Outboards
The choice of engine becomes wider when outboards are an alternative source of power, although their use tends to be restricted to smaller motor cruisers. The modern outboard is a highly reliable piece of equipment and incorporates many of the advantages, in terms of reliability, of a conventional engine. An outboard can be removed from the boat fairly easily for maintenance ashore, which may be an advantage during the winter lay-up. In addition, putting the engine on the back of the boat increases the space available for accommodation or seating inside and means that you have better access to the propellers when you are at sea. An outboard engine provides flexibility in its installation but for some people this is outweighed by an unsophisticated overall impression.

The Sea Drive engine is a cross between a conventional engine and an outboard. It provides a more sophisticated approach to an outboard installation because the boat does not require the transom cutaway for clamping on the engine. The Sea Drive is bolted directly onto the transom, and has all the engine services tidily enclosed, providing space inside the boat. Bear in mind, though, that the Sea Drive increases the overall length of the boat, so that your 25-footer grows to a 27-footer when it comes to handling and marina charges.

FUEL SYSTEMS

A good fuel system is vital to ensure reliable engine operation. You need to know how it is laid out in case things go wrong at sea. Boat builders now recognise the extreme importance of fuel systems and in general take a great deal of trouble to provide sound installation. The fuel system itself, however, will not last for ever; its reliability will depend to a large extent on how well it is maintained. The following is a discussion of the four main

The Sea Drive power units combine the benefits of the outboard and stern drive without taking up space inside the boat.

components of a fuel system; the tank, the filters, the fuel lines and other piping, and the pump.

The Fuel Tank

This is usually made from metal, although if your boat uses diesel, GRP tanks are possible – indeed, some boats have their tanks incorporated into the hull structure. Fuel tanks for petrol are commonly made from steel (brass and copper were the traditional materials). Diesel tanks are commonly made from steel or aluminium. Stainless steel is suitable for both types of fuel.

Fuel tanks are fitted internally with baffles to prevent fuel sloshing about too much at sea. The baffles also strengthen the tank, although they must be positioned to allow fuel to pass freely through to the suction point.

The filler pipe enters the top of the tank; nowadays this is usually a flexible pipe which connects the tank to a deck filling point. The filling point should be outside the superstructure and is usually placed on the side deck. Ideally, it should also be raised above the level of the deck so that if there is any water on deck it will not run down the filler pipe when the cap is opened. With the narrow side decks often found on modern cruisers the filling pipes may be placed in an awkward position, particularly if you have to fill the tank on the side of the boat away from the jetty. The filler tank *must* be outside, however, so that no spillage runs into the accommodation or the bilges. The filler cap should also be clearly marked so that you don't get the fuel and water fillers mixed up. It makes sense to indicate whether you use diesel or petrol just in case somebody else fills up the tank at any time – you could mark the deck with a waterproof pen.

When fuel is taken out of the tank, air has to get in; it is the function of the breather pipe to let this air in. It also lets air out when the tank is being filled – if you are overenthusiastic fuel coming out of the breather pipe will be your first indication that the tank is overfull. For this reason the breather pipe outlet should be below the filler pipe; the normal place is on the topsides just below the fender line. The outlet is covered with a piece of gauze to reduce the possibility of water entering, and a gooseneck inside the line reduces the chance of water trickling down the breather pipe. The size of the breather pipe should be adequate to cope with the fuel filling rate and the pipe should lead from the highest point of the tank.

When filling your tank with diesel the fuel may start 'foaming'. This foam may start to come out of the breather pipe even though the tank is only three-quarters full, so if you are relying on your tank being full make sure that you don't mistake foam for solid fuel and go to sea with less fuel in your tanks than you intended.

The contents of the tank are measured by gauges on most motor cruisers these days, but you cannot rely on these absolutely as they give only an *indication* of what is in the tank. It pays to keep a check on the fuel by working out how much you use per hour at a particular engine rpm – if you know what you put into the tank and what you have taken out you should have a good idea of how much fuel remains. Some fuel systems have a reserve supply you can switch over to if you run out of fuel. This is a very sensible and reassuring arrangement, but again make sure you know how much is in your reserve so that you can plan your tactics accordingly. It is a sensible precaution to fill your tank whenever you get the chance, partly because there is then less chance of running out of fuel, but also because by keeping the tank full you reduce the risk of condensation in the gap between the fuel level and the top of the tank; otherwise water may settle in the bottom of the fuel tank and could cause trouble if left there.

A good fuel installation has a sump in the bottom of the tank which allows water and any sediment to settle. This unhealthy cocktail can be drained off at intervals through a tap in the bottom of the sump until you see good, clean fuel coming out. The fuel suction for the engine is taken from the tank at a point above this sump. In calculating your fuel capacity, therefore, you should allow for the fact that there will always be a certain amount of fuel left in the bottom of the tank which is unusable. The boat builder should be able to advise you about how much usable fuel there is in the tank.

In most cruisers the fuel is carried in tanks which are placed low down in the boat. For the fuel to be transferred to the engine it relies on a pump to suck the fuel through rather than on a gravity feed. In either case there should be a shut-off valve on the fuel line at the point at which it exists from the tank so that if you have a leak or if there is a fire in the engine compartment the fuel can be shut off quickly. Ideally this shut-off valve should be easily accessible and it is a good arrangement to have the spindle of the valve extended so that you can get to it without lifting the hatches.

Filters

Filters are a vital part of the fuel system, particularly for diesel engines. There are usually two filters in the system. One of these is a very fine filter which is incorporated into the engine itself. This filter will need to have its paper element changed at regular intervals as prescribed by the engine manufacturer. The other filter in the system is usually installed by the boat builder and serves the purpose of separating dirt and water from the fuel. Water settles out in the bowl of the filter and dirt is trapped by the filter element. Even if you have a sump in the fuel tank this filter element is essential because, at sea, as the fuel sloshes around, water or dirt in the tank can get stirred up and can find its way up the pipe. The fuel filter should also be readily accessible so that you can quickly check whether there is contamination and clear the system if necessary.

Fuel Lines

Fuel pipes should be made of copper. They should be adequately secured so that there is no possibility of movement which could eventually cause fatigue and allow the pipe to fracture. On a flexibly mounted engine, however, there must be a section of flexible pipe in the system and this should be of the metal braided type for a long and reliable life. Cheaper fuel installations have plastic piping – which may be acceptable provided it is reinforced, but you should check it at very regular intervals and replace annually any flexible plastic piping.

There are risks in using plastic piping, particularly if there is a fire in the engine compartment because the plastic could melt and add fuel to the fire. Leaks in the fuel line, particularly at the joints, are something to watch out for but these will tend to be apparent only when the engine is not running or if you have a

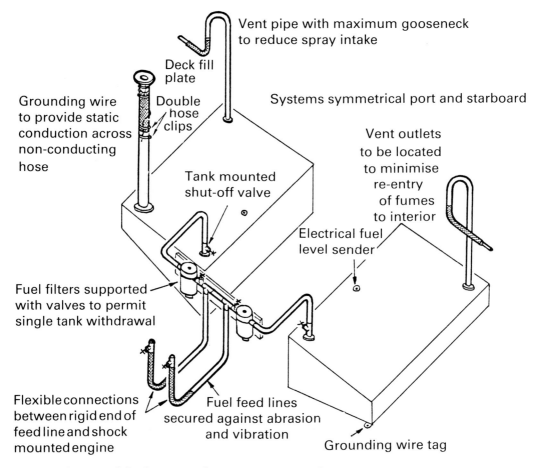

Vent pipe with maximum gooseneck to reduce spray intake

Deck fill plate

Grounding wire to provide static conduction across non-conducting hose

Double hose clips

Systems symmetrical port and starboard

Vent outlets to be located to minimise re-entry of fumes to interior

Tank mounted shut-off valve

Electrical fuel level sender

Fuel filters supported with valves to permit single tank withdrawal

Flexible connections between rigid end of feed line and shock mounted engine

Fuel feed lines secured against abrasion and vibration

Grounding wire tag

A typical fuel system for a twin-engined motor cruiser.

gravity system. At other times the suction in the fuel line may prevent leakage but will also allow air to enter the system, which can rapidly bring a diesel engine to a halt. It is incredibly difficult to trace air leaks in a fuel line on the suction side and the only satisfactory answer if you suspect that this is the case is to install a temporary bypass fuel line from the tank to the engine. If this cures the problem then check out all the joints in the original fuel line very carefully, but if you still cannot find the leak the line will have to be replaced.

In diesel engines there is usually a return fuel line because the fuel system works by supplying more fuel than required to the injectors and the excess then has to be pumped back to the tank.

The return line should be engineered to the same high standards as the rest of the fuel system in order to prevent any leakage.

The fuel system between the pump and the injectors is usually an integral part of the engine and it doesn't pay to interfere with this part of the system in any way. If you want to install a fuel consumption meter the sensor for this should be placed between the initial filter and the fuel pump in order to measure the flow. With a diesel engine, you also have to measure the return flow so that the consumption can be measured by subtracting one from the other, although some systems recycle the return flow through the meter via a small holding tank so that only one flow measurement is required. If you decide to install a fuel consumption meter (and they *are* a worthwhile fitment) follow the manufacturer's instructions very carefully and use good quality materials.

Fuel Pump
The fuel pump is also an integral part of the engine and is generally very reliable. On many engines it incorporates a hand pump which is used to prime the fuel system if you have been working on it. In petrol engines the hand pump is used to refill the carburettor bowl with fuel, whilst in a diesel engine the pump is used to remove air from the system. To do this slightly open one of the joints at the injectors, operate the pump until fuel comes through and then tighten up the joint again. In most cases you will have to go through this routine whenever you adjust the fuel system on a diesel engine in order to remove the air.

Outboard Fuel Systems
The fuel system for an outboard motor is very similar to that described above, and as far as motor cruisers are concerned it usually has a permanently installed tank to which the standard outboard flexible fuel line is connected after the fuel has been passed through a filter system. Outboards may be operated from the portable fuel tanks which are supplied with them. These hold approximately 5 gallons and simplify refuelling if you do not have direct access to a fuel supply.

There are three main problems which can affect the fuel system on outboards over and above the problems normally associated with fuel systems, and these all concern the fuel line. First, there are small non-return valves in the fuel line to alow the priming valve to operate satisfactorily and these can get jammed open by small specks of dirt – hence the need for good filters in the system. Second, the O-ring seals which seal off the snap-on connectors on the fuel line can be damaged: look at these closely and if you see any signs of damage it is time to fit new ones. You will probably be aware of damage if you are unable to get the fuel line up to pressure or if you see leaks from the joints. The third problem arises from kinks or nicks in the rubber fuel line. These may be caused by placing a portable tank on top of the fuel line. Take great care when you lay the fuel line to avoid this problem. It is a sensible precaution to carry a spare fuel line on board in case you run into difficulty.

COOLING SYSTEMS

Air Cooling

Air cooled engines are noisy and require extensive air ducting, which can conflict with the need to keep water out of the boat as it is difficult to keep the ducts watertight. Indeed, it is rare to find them on motor cruisers but for a boat which is used only in very shallow water, such as a canal or a river boat, air cooling can be advantageous in that there are no water connections through the hull so that silt cannot be drawn in to clog the system. An air cooled engine needs to have ducting for the air to be drawn in by the cooling fan and further ducts through which the exhaust can be removed. These ducts should be isolated from the engine compartment so that they do not interfere with the normal air intake of the engine.

Keel Cooling

A keel cooling system is another possibility for river and canal boats. In this kind of system, the engine cooling water flows through tubes attached to the outside of the hull or keel and is cooled by the sea water flowing outside these tubes. The

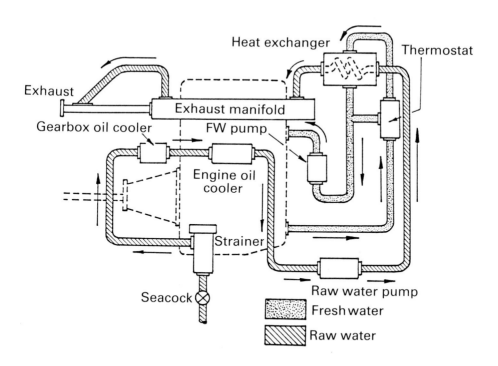

A typical engine cooling system showing the raw seawater and fresh water circuits.

cooled fresh water is then returned to the engine in a closed circuit system. This provides a very good engine cooling system, except that the tubes fitted to the outside of the hull or keel can be vulnerable to damage from debris. This system is not generally used in motor boats, although on larger cruisers it can be used to cool a diesel generator supplying high voltage electric power on board.

Raw Seawater Cooling
This method of engine cooling, in which seawater is passed round the inside of the engine, is now a thing of the past because of inherent corrosion problems and the lack of consistent water temperature. Modern marine engines are fairly highly tuned and therefore incompatible with the vagaries of raw seawater cooling. If you do come across this system, anodes are normally fitted inside the engine to reduce

corrosion. The engine handbook will show their location and they should be checked annually.

Indirect Seawater Cooling

This is the most common type of cooling system and uses raw seawater to cool the fresh water in the fully enclosed engine cooling system. Such a system requires two pumps, one for the seawater and one for the fresh water. The two water circuits meet at the heat exchanger where the sea and fresh water flow through a series of fine adjacent pipes which transfer the heat from the fresh water system to the seawater system.

As engines become more complex, with turbochargers and inter-coolers, the cooling system has a more vital part to play and the complex plumbing which is involved means that you

The hidden depths of the engine compartment. The seacock on the water intake could be made more accessible, but the wiring and piping is well secured to give reliable performance.

need to keep a careful watch on the system. This means checking the flexible pipes and hose clips on a regular basis and also checking for leaks.

Cooling System Problems

Any problems with the cooling system generally occur on the seawater side so here you have to be particularly vigilant. The cooling water is drawn into the boat through a seacock which has a valve to allow the water flow to be shut off. It then passes through a filter before being drawn through the pump and then into the heat exchanger where the raw seawater on one side cools the fresh water of the engine system on the other side. The fresh water system then cools the engine whilst the seawater is passed through a pipe into the exhaust system where it mingles with the exhaust gases to cool these before they pass outboard through the engine exhaust aperture.

The important point to remember when using a seawater system is that any leaks will not only cause problems with the engine cooling but they will allow seawater, possibly in uncontrolled quantities, to enter the inside of the boat which can rapidly put you in danger of sinking. However, you often see a seawater cooling system with the inlet seacock mounted, not unreasonably, in the lowest part of the boat. If one of the pipes fails, allowing water to come into the boat, the seacock is the first thing to be covered. This can make it particularly hard to find and shut off so, as with the fuel shut-off valve, it makes good sense to extend the spindle of the seacock so that it can be reached above decks in any emergency. The filter in the seawater section of the system is designed to stop silt and dirt entering the fine passage in the heat exchanger, so you need to open this and clean it out at regular intervals – but remember to close the seacock before you carry out this operation.

The rest of the cooling system should be made from reinforced piping because it has to withstand the full pressure of the sea. Any leak or weakness will let water into the boat. On planing boats, where the pressure of water can be quite high, a raw seawater cooling system should be engineered with particular care. Whilst boat builders generally install sound systems it is up to you as the owner to make sure that the system is well maintained. Care should be taken over the worm drive clips which secure the flexible pipes; they should be checked at regular intervals both for tightness and corrosion.

The temperature gauge on the dashboard will indicate whether the cooling system is working properly. It only tells part of the story, however, since it is also linked into the fresh water side of the system. The cooling system is possibly the most neglected area of motor cruiser engine installations, yet it can cause major headaches if you do neglect it. Not only will the engine overheat and stop running but it may also cause the boat to sink. Time spent checking the cooling system is time well spent.

EXHAUST SYSTEMS

In the most common type of exhaust which uses water injection the exhaust system is linked to the cooling system. The seawater from the cooling system is injected into the exhaust pipe when it leaves the engine. The exhaust pipe flows downwards so that the water cannot flow back into the engine. As the water mixes with the exhaust gases it performs the vital task of cooling them. The exhaust pipe usually consists of a large diameter rubber tube which is convenient because of the ease with which it can be installed. However, if the rubber piping is exposed to the full heat of the exhaust gases it may catch fire or at least melt and cause a fire in the engine room.

This demonstrates the vital role played by the cooling system, and the first noticeable effect of an interruption in the cooling water supply may well be a smouldering exhaust pipe. Because the exhaust pipe contains both the exhaust gases and seawater, the pipe itself needs to be in good condition and should be checked during each annual overhaul, with particular attention being paid to the securing clips and the location of the pipe in the boat.

The water which is injected into the exhaust helps to reduce noise, although some installations have an additional silencer incorporated into the system to reduce the level even further.

These silencers are specially designed to accommodate both the gas and the water flow, and like the rest of the exhaust system they need to be checked at regular intervals. This is not always easy where the exhaust piping passes below the aft accommodation. The exhaust pipe's route should be carefully planned by the boat builder so that water cannot flow back up through the pipe, particularly when the boat is going astern. The pressure of the exhaust gases is usually adequate to prevent this, and you are rarely going astern quickly enough to build up any sort of water pressure, anyway.

ELECTRICAL SYSTEMS

The electrical system on a motor cruiser probably causes more headaches than anything else. As we try to build more and more of the comforts of home into a boat the electrical system becomes more and more complex. It requires considerable care and dedication to install it properly in the first place and equal care to maintain it in good condition. The electrical system is not only important for providing the comforts of home on board but it also plays a vital role in supplying power for the electronic navigation equipment, navigation lights and bilge pumps, all of which are important factors in the safety of the boat. In fact, the electrical system in a modern motor boat is now just as essential as the engines. Make sure that all the electrical components are kept well away from seawater and that the wiring is properly secured to avoid damage.

Batteries
The basis of the electrical system is the battery into which the power is supplied from the engine-driven alternator and from which the power is drawn to supply the main distribution board and thence the various units in the electrical system. On modern motor cruisers double battery installations are widely used; one battery is reserved simply for engine starting and the other supplies all the auxiliary systems. Both batteries can be charged from one alternator through a blocking diode system which switches the charge to the battery which is most in need of it. This is a good system because it means that you should always

have a fully charged battery available for starting the engine. Once started, the engine can then supply a charge to the other battery if necessary.

With twin engines a double battery installation is not always adopted. You simply have one battery for each engine, leaving you to decide which battery to use to supply the auxiliary circuits. With such a system you have to be a little more disciplined about how you use the electrical power to ensure that you still have enough power left for starting the engine. Such a system is usually fitted with a paralleling switch, which allows two engine batteries to be linked temporarily so that you can use the power left in both batteries to start at least one engine. You should then be able to get the whole system up and running. Since hand starting of engines is now virtually a thing of the past, the electrical engine starting system is vital.

The batteries themselves should be well secured in trays so that any acid spillage does not corrode vital parts of the boat. The batteries should be bolted or clamped in position so that there is no possibility of movement. The large cables which supply power from the battery to the engine starter do not take kindly to movement so they should be well secured, although a degree of movement is necessary if the engine is flexibly mounted.

Wiring
The wiring throughout the boat should also be well secured. Particularly vulnerable areas such as bulkheads or sharp corners which could lead to wear on the insulation should be protected. The connections are always a vulnerable point in any electrical system and these need to be carefully engineered to give reliable performance. They should also be well protected from water because this is how corrosion often starts. Any electrical wiring outside the boat must go through watertight glands, both where it passes through the deck and where it enters the equipment such as sidelights; these areas should always be part of your annual inspection routine.

Distribution and Fuses
At the distribution board the main supply from the batteries is divided into a number of circuits, each of which is protected by a

fuse or a breaker. Breakers are preferable to fuses because you can bring the circuit back into operation simply by flicking the switch – provided, of course, that there is no permanent damage. On a dark night when you have lost your navigation lights flicking a switch will be much easier than the tedious

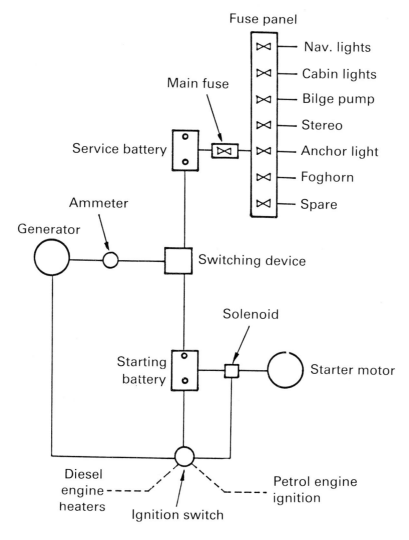

Layout of a typical wiring system on a motor cruiser. All of the links are made with double wiring and the distribution board is likely to be more comprehensive than shown here.

business of changing a fuse in the dark. The circuit board fuses or breakers are often supplemented by fuses on individual pieces of equipment. It pays to have spare fuses of all types on board and to know just where they are located. You can be sure that when a fuse blows it will be at the most inconvenient time – a quick repair could get you out of a difficult situation. On some electronic equipment, the fuse may be inside the case rather than on it, which means a dismantling job to find it. Other equipment will have fuses installed in the line; these need to be identified so that you can locate them in the dark.

Problem Areas
Weak points in the electrical circuit are often found underneath the dashboard where there is always a great mass of wiring. Water can leak through the dashboard instruments or panels if they are not properly sealed and cause all sorts of trouble underneath. The other problem area is the engine room – where high temperatures, water, oil and fuel can all provide a very unhealthy environment for the electrical systems. There should be no loose wiring in the engine compartment and as far as is practical all the wiring should be as high as possible. Fittings such as switches and control boxes should be well away from hatches and other areas where water can get in.

Electrical circuits on boats are either 12 or 24 volt DC, depending on the voltage of the engine systems. With the demand for home comforts and the availability of power supplies alongside in marinas, many boats are now able to be connected to shore power, which can bring high voltage alternating current on board. This current may be lethal if it is not handled properly – extra care needs to be taken in the installation of these high voltage circuits and regular checking is essential. Unless fully waterproof fittings are used all the connections in the circuit should be well protected from water and a fully fused and protected control box is essential.

Because of the demand for high voltage equipment even cruisers of around 30 feet (9 metres) in length may be fitted with an auxiliary generator to supply this voltage at sea. The same principles as with a shore-based high voltage system apply and, obviously, it should be kept totally separate from any low voltage circuits. The only possible connection between the two may be through a battery charger which allows the high voltage system to supply a charging current to the low voltage batteries to keep them in tip-top condition. Battery chargers are largely automatic these days and can be left to their own devices for long periods, but they should be installed where there is a good circulation of air to carry away excess heat.

The batteries found on motor cruisers will give off hydrogen during the charging operation. Hydrogen is a very explosive gas but since it is lighter than air it normally dissipates quite freely, provided there is some form of ventilation above the batteries. You are not likely to encounter problems with hydrogen unless your motor cruiser has a bank of several batteries. In this case some form of spark-proof fan to provide ventilation over the batteries and to remove the accumulation of hydrogen gas may be necessary.

NOISE REDUCTION

Noise is irritating, and on motor boats there are many potential sound generators. The hull banging in waves is the most obvious. The fixtures and fittings in the accommodation can also contribute considerably to noise levels. However, the engine probably presents the largest potential source of noise on board. Whilst boat builders are getting better at reducing noise levels, you can often improve things quite a bit. Noise reduction is expensive, though, and inevitably adds weight to the boat, both factors which may persuade you that sound levels are not too much of an intrusion!

There are three ways to reduce noise. First, try to isolate the sound source. Second, try to insulate against the noise by establishing some form of barrier between you and the sound. Third, try to damp out the sound.

Isolation of engine noise is usually carried out by the builder and involves putting the engine on flexible mounts and using flexible couplings in the propeller shaft. In addition to direct noise reduction this also helps to reduce vibrations in the hull structure caused by engine vibration. Hull vibration itself can be reduced by applying damping material to the vibrating panels.

The damping material in effect alters the frequency of vibration of the panels so that it no longer corresponds with that of the engine.

First you have to find the panels which are vibrating. They are easily recognised if they are deck or accommodation panels. Doors and other similar fittings can be particularly susceptible to vibration. Try applying a stiffener to the rear of the panel or apply specialised damping material (available from sound-proofing specialists). To identify the culprit panels go round the boat when it is underway, pressing on particular panels to see whether this eliminates vibration noise. This can be a long and tedious process but a quiet boat will give you a lot more pleasure.

The second method of reducing noise involves insulating the engine compartment by lining it with soundproofing material. The bulkheads and the hatches or panels above the engine usually receive this treatment. To do the job properly the sides of the boat should also be lined with soundproofing material. It is not usually necessary to soundproof the bottom of the engine compartment because the seawater outside does a pretty good job of damping out the sound; you are only concerned with putting a barrier between yourself and the sound generators.

If the exhaust strikes an offensive note you may like to fit a silencer in the exhaust line, but it is usually the noise transmitted directly from the engine which is the main culprit, particularly if the engine is mounted underneath the saloon floor or cockpit deck where the crew spend most of their time when at sea.

PROPULSION SYSTEMS

You can put all the power you like into a boat but unless you can transmit that power to the water and develop thrust it will be to little effect. The propulsion system and propellers are critical to the operation of a motor cruiser; it will also improve your driving if you understand what is going on below the water line. There is a wide choice of propulsion systems for motor cruisers, all with differing advantages and disadvantages.

Conventional Propulsion

Displacement motor cruisers usually opt for what might be called the conventional propulsion system where the gearbox is linked to the propeller by a straight shaft. The gearbox allows you to select ahead, neutral and astern gears for manoeuvring but it almost invariably also incorporates a reduction gear to reduce the speed of the propeller shaft to less than the speed of the engine. For maximum efficiency on a displacement boat the propeller should be as large as possible. A large propeller turns more slowly so the engine speed has to be reduced by the gearbox.

For maximum efficiency the propeller shaft should be as near to the horizontal as possible. A near horizontal shaft line can be achieved on displacement boats, where the propeller is in an aperture at the stern. If the propellers are placed below the hull, as is generally the case with planing boats, the shaft has to be placed at an angle of up to 15 degrees from the horizontal. This means that the propellers are also working at an angle of 15 degrees to the horizontal, so that there is an immediate loss of efficiency. The angle of the propeller thrust has an effect on the trim of the boat — something the designer has to take into account.

In a conventional system the propeller shaft passes through the hull by means of a stern gland, which supports the shaft and also creates an effective seal between the rotating shaft and the fixed hull to prevent water coming in. The stern gland will need regular inspection to make sure that water is not seeping in (although a few drops of water are acceptable). You should also feel the stern gland when the boat is running to ensure that it is not too hot. If you can't keep your hand on the stern gland then it is probably running too hot, which means that the sealing material is binding on the shaft. If this happens slacken off the stern gland slightly. A properly adjusted gland should seal the joint completely when the shaft is not turning. The gland is adjusted by tightening or slackening the nuts; it is important to do this evenly so that the gland is parallel to the shaft. Any persistent leaking from the stern gland which cannot be taken up by adjustment usually indicates that there is wear in the propeller shaft bearings. This means it is time to slip the boat and check things out.

The propeller shaft is supported at the inboard end by the gearbox, which also takes the thrust from the propeller shaft. If the engine and gearbox are flexibly mounted there should be a flexible joint where the shaft emerges from the gearbox to accommodate the relative movement of the propeller shaft and engine. This joint is usually of the rubber torsional type and requires no maintenance.

Where the propeller shaft emerges from the stern of the boat the stern tube also incorporates the rear propeller shaft bearing. This may be lubricated with grease which is forced into the shaft through a special greaser, or you may have a water lubricated Cutlass bearing, whereby the water is channelled into the bearing through small scoops incorporated into the bearing housing outside the hull. It is important to keep these scoops free of barnacles and other marine growth. They should be carefully treated with anti-fouling paint and cleaned whenever the boat is slipped.

Where the propellers are under the hull the stern tube is usually there just to effect a seal, although it can also act as a bearing. The rear bearing is usually mounted on a P or an A bracket immediately in front of the propeller. With this type of bearing water lubrication is almost invariably used; the water flows straight through the bearing from one end to the other. Water lubricated bearings are usually made from hard rubber so the propeller shaft should never be turned under engine power when the boat is out of the water because the bearing will quickly become very hot without the essential water lubrication.

Stern Drive Units
When conventional propulsion systems are used on planing boats the steep shaft angle interrupts the flow of water to the propeller and reduces efficiency. In an attempt to overcome these deficiencies and to simplify installation work the stern drive unit was developed. Here the engine is placed right in the stern of the boat and is close coupled to the stern drive unit by a short horizontal shaft. Within the drive leg the drive unit is taken through two 90 degree turns so that the propeller shaft

emerges at the bottom of the unit in a horizontal line. Usually the gearbox is incorporated into the stern drive so that all the propulsion requirements are covered by a single unit. These units have achieved excellent reliability with reduced maintenance.

Stern drive units also offer the facility for the leg to be tilted, even at sea, which means you have access to the propellers in case of damage or fouling by ropes or debris. Tilting is also a useful feature if the boat has to be beached or loaded onto a trailer. Stern drives make for a tidy, compact installation which gives good propulsive efficiency. The only maintenance necessary on a routine basis is checking of the oil level. This can be done either with a dipstick inside the hull or by removing a level plug in the leg itself when the boat is out of the water. Because the stern drive leg is constructed from aluminium, the

It is possible to trail smaller motor cruisers, but stern drives or outboards are essential as they can be tilted when trailing.

leg may be sensitive to corrosion, so anodes are usually attached to reduce the problem. Check these annually and replace if they have been eroded.

High Performance Drive Systems

Other propulsion systems used on motor cruisers are applicable mainly to high performance craft. The Arneson drive and the Levi drive employ surface piercing propellers where the shaft emerges from the bottom of the transom in an almost horizontal line. When the boat is on the plane only the bottom half of the propeller is in the water, which reduces the drag associated with normal propulsion systems and gives greater efficiency. The Levi drive and some of the other drive systems of this type now appearing on the market use a propeller shaft with a fixed angle, whereas with the Arneson drive the shaft is articulated and can be moved both vertically to adjust the depth of immersion of the propeller and horizontally to adjust the steering.

PROPELLERS

Even after years of development, propeller design seems to remain as much an art as a science and when you look at the variables involved it is easy to see why. A propeller can vary in diameter, in pitch (the distance covered in one turn of the propeller), in the number of blades and in the blade area and shape. There is an almost infinite variety of propeller configurations. The propeller you use is bound to be something of a compromise because it has to work at both high and low speeds and its size may be limited by the hull shape. The propeller also has to be matched to the engine power characteristics.

In most cases, a boat builder will spend some time experimenting with and developing the right propeller for a boat. However, bear in mind that the choice of propeller will depend to a degree on the *way* you use the boat, so that if you want maximum speed it may be best to switch to a propeller with a larger pitch, although you will have to accept that this will reduce other aspects of performance. For instance, you might find that you have difficulty getting the boat onto the plane with a heavy load when using a high performance propeller. If you always carry a lot of passengers you might want to opt for a smaller pitch propeller to compensate for this. The same applies if you use your boat for water skiing, where good acceleration is just as important as top speed. This can be achieved by a smaller pitch or perhaps a smaller diameter propeller. Having said all this, changing one aspect of propeller design usually affects others, so you should only change from the standard propeller if your needs are specialised.

Propeller Tuning

With outboards and stern drives, changing the propeller is a comparatively simple operation because of the wide choice available. If you can find a friendly dealer who will allow you to try alternative propellers you can experiment to a certain extent, varying the pitch and possibly the diameter by small amounts to judge the effect on performance. What you are trying to achieve is a situation in which the engine is running close to its maximum rpm with the throttles wide open and with the boat carrying its normal load. If the engines go over the safe rpm limit the propeller is probably too small – you will have to constantly watch your rev counter but you will certainly get better acceleration. If the engines do not reach their full rpm the boat will be sluggish because full power is not being developed. This probably means the propellers are too large.

Because of their vital role in transmitting engine power to the water it pays to keep the propellers in good condition. A propeller which has nicks or other deformities around the edges of the blade will be less efficient. The same is true if you let marine growth develop. Keeping the propellers clean and polished, and touched up where necessary with a file or by very gently tapping with a hammer to remove marine growth, can help to maintain propeller efficiency.

Propeller Operation

If you think about the flow of water in which most propellers have to operate, it is quite easy to see why propellers are not always as efficient as they might be. In front of the propeller the water flow may be interrupted by the shaft or by the propeller brackets or, on a stern drive leg, by the drive housing, so that by the time the water actually reaches the propeller it is not flowing evenly. In spite of this uneven flow the propeller still manages to work remarkably efficiently. In fact, it is mainly the blades on the bottom half of the propeller turn which do the work, leaving the blades on the top half to work in the dirty flow of water. This has led to the development of the surface piercing propeller which keeps just the bottom blades in the water doing work in a clean, steady flow of water whilst the top blades offer no resistance.

Surface piercing propellers are very effective at speeds of over 35 knots. In fact, when you trim your stern drive leg out, to a certain extent you are bringing the propeller into a surface piercing mode. These propellers are fine when the boat is up and running fast, but because the propeller is fully immersed as you start to come up onto the plane this can put great stress on the engine and on the propellers themselves. This means that surface piercing propellers have to be specially designed for the job.

MAINTENANCE

Proper maintenance of the engine and propulsion system is vital. Before you go to sea, as a matter of routine check the engine oil and coolant levels as well as making a general check of the engine compartment. Get into the habit of turning off the water intake seacocks every time you come into harbour so that you are forced to go down into the engine compartment to open these before leaving. This will also give you the opportunity to look around the engine compartment to make sure that all is in order, everything is stowed away and the levels are correct. If you do turn off the seacocks it is wise to hang a notice over the throttles or ignition switches just to remind yourself that the seacocks are turned off. Otherwise you will find the engine temperature rising alarmingly because there is no cooling water.

Apart from keeping everything as clean as possible this is all the routine maintenance that should be necessary, and you could probably go most of the season without doing very much more than changing the engine and gearbox oil at regular intervals, checking the battery acid levels, and thoroughly checking the engine compartment electrical system, as well as the fuel filters from time to time.

If you carry out this routine on a monthly basis you should be able to pre-empt any problems which might occur whilst you are out at sea. Do not ignore any signs of trouble, such as an oil or water leak, signs of slight movement around the fuel tank or corrosion in electrical connections, because these problems will not get better on their own. Even if you can't fix the problem straight away, at least make a note of it so that it is not forgotten.

These monthly maintenance checks are a good way of getting to know your boat better and ensuring no problems are developing. The more you study the workings of your boat, the better you will cope if things go wrong at sea. Keep a list of defects which do not require urgent attention, so that you can attend to them at the annual re-fit. This is when the boat is taken out of the water so that the stern gear can be inspected for wear and tear.

At this stage check the propeller shaft to make sure there is no undue movement in the bearing. Carry out the same check on the rudder bearings simply by trying to move the rudder from side to side. If wear is detected in these areas it is likely to get worse, so if you want to enjoy relaxed cruising during the next season fit replacements even though the wear may not seem too bad at the time.

Every time the boat is out of the water the oil levels in the stern drive legs should be checked. The zinc anodes, which are fitted to reduce electrolytic corrosion, should also be examined and replaced if they are eroded. When the boat is laid up for the winter you must either put anti-freeze in the fresh water of the cooling system or drain the system completely to prevent it freezing. Water tanks and hot water heating systems should also be drained during the winter months if the boat is not in use. If you use the boat during the winter you should perhaps consider a low level of heating which can be run off the mains supply from the marina to prevent any problems with freezing and also to keep the boat dry during the damp winter months.

Maintenance is really a matter of common sense as far as the machinery goes, but there is a growing tendency in the design of motor cruisers to hide the machinery away and make it as unobtrusive as possible. This is fine from the point of view of comfort but when it extends to making it difficult to gain access to the engines, as happens in some designs, you can have a situation where 'out of sight, out of mind' applies. You will only become aware of your neglect when you are let down out at sea and have to call for help. The golden rule about going to sea is that you should be self-sufficient and not rely on others to bail you out; care and attention to maintenance of the machinery will go a long way to achieving this end.

11 · Safety and security

We have looked at all the aspects of running and operating a boat and if you get all of this right then you should not have any problems with safety. Your boat should operate reliably and, as the skipper, you should anticipate problems and deal with them before they become serious. However, throughout this book it is emphasised that when you are out at sea you are on your own, and the prudent seaman always keeps something up his sleeve to cope with emergencies. When things have gone badly wrong it is nice to have the possibility of one more chance to get out of trouble; this is where safety equipment comes in.

There is no denying the importance of safety equipment and it would be foolish to think of operating a boat without it, but just putting safety equipment on board is not the answer when things go wrong. Like everything else on board, you have to know how to operate the safety equipment, what it can and can't do and, above all, the conditions and situations in which you ought to use it. In this chapter we will be looking at a wide variety of equipment to cope with emergencies of one sort or another. It is all vital equipment but none of it guarantees your safety. Only you as the skipper can do that by good driving, preparation and maintenance.

LIFERAFTS

A liferaft is often regarded as the most essential piece of safety equipment because if the boat sinks it will give you another chance of survival. But you have to bear in mind that it is a rather fragile haven if you have to abandon ship and you should

The layout of a flybridge cruiser. Note the liferaft stowage, ready for instant use, yet out of the way.

only use it if there is *no other alternative*. It has been demonstrated time and time again that it is better to stay with your boat as long as possible rather than take to the liferaft. However, it is reassuring to have this option ready for use in dire emergencies.

Liferafts are contained in either a soft valise or a rigid GRP case. The latter is by far the best on a motor cruiser because it gives the liferaft good protection, particularly against the movement of the boat. On a planing motor cruiser the best stowage is somewhere in the cockpit where the liferaft is ready for immediate and easy use, whilst on a displacement motor cruiser you could stow it on the foredeck, although here it can be vulnerable to water washing over the deck. Stowage here might also obstruct the view from the wheelhouse. A protected position in the rear of the boat is best in both circumstances, but remember that when you come to use the liferaft the boat may be rolling violently and you should ensure that it is stowed in a position where it can be launched in such conditions. You can stow a liferaft in a locker when you are in harbour for security, but always remember to have it out on deck ready for use when you are at sea. It should be stowed with a quick release securing strap and *always* remember to tie the painter onto a strong point on the boat such as a mooring cleat. In an emergency you will almost certainly forget to do this when you put the liferaft over the side; it would be very sad to see your raft drifting away just when you really need it.

Having a liferaft is an act of faith because you have to assume that it is going to work when you tug the painter to activate the inflation mechanism. You should, if possible, attend a demonstration of liferaft inflation so that you have some idea what is inside the white box which you carefully stow every time you go to sea. It helps a great deal in an emergency to know what is involved in inflating a liferaft. You should also practise climbing into it so that you are better prepared for the situation in any emergency.

Your liferaft will need to be serviced every year and you may be able to make an arrangement with the service station to inflate it before you send it back so that you will have some idea just what your particular raft is like.

TENDERS AS AN ALTERNATIVE

Liferafts are expensive and it can be difficult to find suitable stowage for one on board. An alternative worth considering is upgrading your tender to make it suitable for use in emergencies. This can usually only be done if you have an inflatable tender, and if it is going to be suitable for emergency use it should either be carried fully inflated or be fitted with an inflation gas bottle so that inflation can be carried out very quickly if required. In an open inflatable at sea you could quickly succumb to exposure so some form of protective canopy over the tender is essential if it is going to double as a liferaft. Many manufacturers of inflatables now offer an upgrading kit which comprises gas bottle inflation, a protective canopy and a bag of essential survival equipment, all of which you need if your tender is to be suitable for liferaft duty.

USING LIFERAFTS IN EMERGENCIES

If you have to use your liferaft – and remember it should only be used as a *last* resort – you would normally put it over the lee side of the boat. A tug on the painter will initiate the inflation procedure, which should take about a minute to complete, although you can start climbing aboard before this. There is an emergency pack on board which will meet your very basic requirements, but you can keep a grab bag readily available in the wheelhouse with essentials such as flares, extra food and water, warm clothing and similar items which could be useful in such circumstances. Such a bag can be particularly useful if you are cruising in remote areas where help might not be immediately available if you have to abandon ship.

Once aboard the liferaft you should stay attached to the boat for as long as possible, particularly if you have managed to send out a distress signal. Be ready to cut or slip the painter at very short notice if the boat shows signs of imminent sinking. A knife is fitted to the liferaft for this purpose. Once adrift it is important to deploy the sea anchor which you will find in the emergency pack; this will stop your drift and keep you somewhere in the vicinity of the position from which you indicated your distress, so that rescuers will be able to find you in the shortest possible time. There are seasickness tablets in the emergency pack which all of the crew should take even if they are not normally prone to seasickness.

LIFE JACKETS

Unlike liferafts, life jackets and lifebuoys have a vital role to play in the day-to-day operation of your motor cruiser and the US Coast Guard has a requirement for certain types of life jackets on US powerboats. Whilst not essential wear, a lifejacket can provide flotation if you find yourself unexpectedly overboard. Some people like to wear one all the time when they are at sea and there is nothing wrong with this. When you wear a life jacket is largely a matter of personal choice, although if you get caught out in difficult conditions where the boat itself could be at risk then it is a sensible precaution for the skipper to order the crew to put on life jackets. Similarly, if you had to go onto the foredeck, work in the cockpit or perhaps clear a line from the propeller, wearing a life jacket is a sensible precaution. If somebody goes over the side it at least gives them immediate flotation so that there is not quite the same panic when you try to pick them up. For children, a life jacket should be considered essential at all times.

Life jackets come in three main forms. The first has full inherent buoyancy with foam or may have a combination of foam and air inflation. Life jackets of this type tend to be a little unwieldy and restrictive to wear but they will keep you afloat and the right way up if you go overboard in an unconscious state. The second type also has full inherent buoyancy and is worn rather like a waistcoat. It will keep you afloat but offers no guarantee to float you face upwards. Finally, there is the fully inflatable type of life jacket with either oral or gas bottle inflation, which is unobtrusive to wear but relies on being inflated before it is effective. From this you will see that the life jacket which is most effective in the water is the one which is most restrictive and could hamper your movements around the boat, perhaps even making you more likely to fall in the water. Selecting the correct life jacket for the job is difficult. For children the buoyancy aid type is probably best because they are more comfortable and can be worn at all times. For adults, the fully inflatable version is probably the best compromise and they certainly have the merit of taking up very little stowage space on board and can be kept in the wheelhouse ready for immediate use in any emergency. Coast Guard requirements insist that life jackets are carried on board. It is up to you to use them intelligently.

LIFEBUOYS

Lifebuoys are carried on board in readiness to throw to any crew member who falls overboard. They should be stowed where they can be used immediately and easily because when you need one you will certainly need it in a hurry. If possible, they should be easy to reach from the steering position and for use at night at least one lifebuoy should be fitted with an emergency light which comes on automatically when the lifebuoy hits the water. If a crew member falls overboard when you are motoring, although you will not be able to get the lifebuoy near him throw it over anyway as it can act as a useful marker when turning back, particularly at night.

DISTRESS SIGNALS

There are many ways of indicating that you are in trouble at sea and radio is probably the most important. However, your radio may cease to function in an emergency and distress signals are an important back-up. These come in three main types, smoke flares, parachute flares and hand flares, and each has a particular function.

Smoke flares are for use in daylight and when activated emit clouds of orange smoke. On a calm day they can be visible for several miles, but in a fresh breeze the smoke disperses very rapidly and is much less visible. Hand flares are primarily for use at night and the distress type emit a brilliant red light which can be visible for several miles. However, because they are handheld and low down this visibility could be restricted by the low horizon. Parachute flares, on the other hand, are ejected skywards by a rocket, bursting at around 1000 feet (300 metres) where a parachute opens and the flare descends slowly, lasting for about 30 seconds. Parachute flares are a highly effective distress signal and even in daylight can provide a much more visible means of indicating your problem than smoke flares.

Using Flares

Just buying the correct flares and stowing them on board will not bring help automatically. Firing flares requires thought and care. Both the hand and smoke flares should be let off on the *lee side* of the boat. The hand flares, in particular, tend to spew out red hot ash, so hold them out at arm's length and at a slight angle so that the ash drops in the water.

To anyone who has not fired a parachute flare before, it can be something of a frightening experience, so attend a demonstration if you get the chance. The important thing to remember is to hold the tube firmly in your hands because there is a slight recoil as the rocket goes off. Make sure that there is no rigging or other obstruction above you so that the rocket has a clear path skywards. Because they are so effective you should have at least four parachute flares on board and these should be backed up with the same number of hand flares and a couple of smoke flares.

The normal shelf life of flares is two years and in most cases the expiry date is stamped on the outside. Disposing of time expired flares can be quite a problem and you must *never* fire them off because you could unwittingly alert the emergency services and start a search. The dealer from whom you buy flares will normally advise about disposal arrangements for old flares.

FIRE EXTINGUISHERS

Fire is always a potential hazard on board a motor boat because of the fuels which are carried, so adequate fire extinguishers are essential. These can be divided into two categories; those that are used to extinguish fires in the engine compartment and those that can cope with fires in the wheelhouse and accommodation.

Engine Room Fires

Because the engine compartment is largely enclosed, any fire in this area can be controlled simply by blanketing the compartment with a fire extinguishing gas. Systems are available for this to be done automatically, whereby a heat sensor automatically sets off the extinguishers. However desirable an automatic system of this type may appear, a manually activated system is to be preferred. The latter system works by having a heat detector in the engine compartment which activates an alarm at the dashboard to indicate that there is a fire.

This means that before activating the manual fire extinguishers from the dashboard, the engines can be stopped and the fuel shut off so that there is a much better chance of the fire actually being extinguished. If you feel there is time, all the air inlets to the engine compartment should also be blanked off and any exhaust fans should certainly be switched off.

With any engine compartment fire extinguishing system you have only one chance to extinguish the fire, and unless you take these precautions beforehand the fire may continue and you will have a major problem on your hands. The manual system gives a much better chance of getting things right and also reduces the chance of false alarms activating the system unnecessarily.

Accommodation Fires

For fires in the accommodation, a series of fire extinguishers placed at strategic points will cover most eventualities. The fire extinguishers should be placed just inside exit doors so that you can grab the extinguisher and fight the fire whilst keeping your escape route open. Most fire extinguishers for boats these days use vaporising liquid, either BCF or BTM. Extinguishers between 1.5 kg (3 lb) and 2.5 kg (5 lb) are best for boat use, anything larger is difficult to handle – you should be able to use them one-handed so that you have one hand to hold on with if the boat is rolling around. Like all emergency equipment you should familiarise yourself with the use of fire extinguishers beforehand because you will not have time to read the instructions when a fire starts.

The galley area is one of the major fire risk areas on board, and here an asbestos fire blanket is a good precaution for coping with localised fires. They can be used to smother a fire quickly without the mess associated with the use of fire extinguishers and are equally valuable if someone's clothing catches fire.

At sea you are surrounded by water, which is a good fire extinguishing medium for everything except fuel fires. The problem lies in getting the water to the seat of the fire, but if you have run out of extinguishers then seawater is the next best thing. Do not use seawater if the boat has 110 or 220 volt circuits which are live.

RAILS AND SAFETY HARNESSES

Normally when you are at sea the crew on board will be confined to the cockpit. There is no need to go up onto the foredeck, except perhaps in very fine weather when this is often used as a sunbathing area. The cockpit on most motor cruisers is well protected with bulwarks or rails and provides a comparatively secure environment in which guests can enjoy the pleasures of the trip. The foredeck is not so secure, although most boats are provided with rails of either wire and stanchion or the now more popular stainless steel tubing to offer a measure of protection.

However, whilst you will normally only use the foredeck when mooring in harbour you can find yourself in situations where you have to go up there in difficult conditions, perhaps when using the anchor in an emergency or when being taken in tow if you have an engine failure. Whilst the rails themselves provide a measure of security, good handholds are essential, particularly at the side deck area adjacent to the wheelhouse. The narrow side decks and often low rails can make this a vulnerable area to manoeuvre past, particularly in harbour, and if you feel a sense of insecurity then extra handholds are a must.

On the foredeck there is often little to hold on to except the rails themselves, making you both exposed and vulnerable. The rails can provide a measure of security but if you have to go on the foredeck in difficult conditions a safety harness can give added security. The safety harness line has to be clipped on to a strong point such as a cleat – the rails are rarely strong enough. Using a safety harness in this way can restrict movement because you must keep the line fairly short for it to be effective. However, its use is strongly recommended in difficult conditions.

During normal running you will want to wear a safety harness, partly because if you go overboard on the end of a safety line there is always the risk that you will end up close to the propeller. Secondly, if you go overboard at any speed above about 8 knots wearing a safety harness you risk serious injury from the sudden jolt as the line comes tight. A life jacket is probably a better bet because if you do go overboard you will fall clear and can be picked up again. If you are simply looking for security when seated in the cockpit without work to do the seat harnesses suggested earlier are a much better solution than a safety harness.

NAVIGATION LIGHTS AND HORN

You are required by law to carry navigation lights and a horn, or some other means of making noise. Both of these are required to indicate your presence to other people either at night or in poor visibility. The size, colour and power of lights are prescribed by the International Regulations for the Prevention of Collision at Sea, and the skipper of any motor cruiser should have a good working knowledge of these rules. Any reputable boat builder will fit navigation lights, although there is a tendency to bend the rules to a certain extent as far as their location is concerned. Basically, a motor cruiser should have four navigation lights. Looked at in plain view, a white light should show from ahead for 112½ degrees on either side, and a second lower white light aft fills in the gap left by this light. The green and red sidelights, green to starboard and red to port, shine from right ahead over an arc of 112½ degrees on their respective sides. The masthead light should be visible for 3 miles and the remaining lights for 2 miles, but for your own interests you want to be as visible as possible and the brighter the lights the more easily other craft will see you.

One of the biggest problems with navigation lights at night is that the masthead light, shining forward, lights up the foredeck and the hand rails, destroying your night vision. To a certain extent this can be cured by fitting a plate underneath the light so that the foredeck area is in shadow but this is not always effective. The only other real solution is to paint the offending areas of the deck and rails matt black, which is not always aesthetically pleasing. These reflections can be a particular problem when you are coming into a dark harbour with few lights and there is always the temptation to switch the lights off to give better visibility. You do this at your peril because you may well come across other boats doing the same thing, which can only lead to trouble.

The horn has many functions on board but should be used only when really needed. On some rivers and canals horn signals are used to request bridge opening or when approaching locks, but the prime function of the horn is for use in poor visibility when you are required by law to sound a long blast every minute. If this is going to be an effective fog signal you do need a good horn and it should be one which will stand up well to seawater. Even though it is required by law the use of sounding fog signals in poor visibility has diminished, partly because of the advent of radar and partly because fog signals are very difficult to hear over the engine noise. However, you do have legal obligations and the person in a small sailing boat may be very grateful if he can hear your fog signal, even if you are unable to hear those of other boats easily.

An alternative to the electrical type of fog signal is an electronic loud hailer. These are available both for speaking and for sounding fog signals, and when used in the latter mode are often fitted with automatic timing devices which do the job for you. The availability of combined loud hailer and fog signal is quite useful but it is something that should be used very sparingly in harbour to avoid annoyance to other water uses.

FIRST AID

In keeping with the need to be self-sufficient at sea the ability to deal with personal accidents on board is vital. In the early stages of any injury to one of your crew you are very much on your own at sea and a comprehensive first aid kit is very important. In addition to having suitable equipment for treating cuts and burns and other minor problems you should also be prepared to cope with more major injuries such as severe burns and broken limbs. Standard first aid kits are available which are specifically designed for motor cruiser use or you can go to a friendly chemist and ask him to make up a suitable kit for you, explaining just what your requirements are.

With any type of serious injury on board it is very reassuring to be able to get medical advice. In most countries it is possible to be put directly in contact with a doctor on shore via your onboard radio. With this contact you can describe the injuries and get advice about treatment. The radio can also be used to get medical help to you quickly if the accident is severe enough to justify it.

Having somebody aboard who is trained in basic first aid is excellent because even on the best run boat accidents will happen. If this expertise is not available at least make sure that you have a first aid manual on board so that you have some idea how to cope with an accident.

Seasickness is very debilitating and its effects should be taken very seriously. Any first aid kit on board should have seasickness tablets, although these tend to have little effect once the person is affected by seasickness. The tablets need to be taken in anticipation of the problem rather than as a cure. There are available on the market sticking plaster patches which are positioned behind the ear, allowing chemicals to be absorbed through the skin; these can be used after the onslaught of seasickness because the cure is not absorbed through the stomach and therefore it has a good chance of being effective. Unfortunately this cure for seasickness is only available on prescription in most countries, but if you are a serious sufferer then this might be the solution. Another alternative cure favoured by some are Sea Bands. These bands are worn in a special position on the wrists and work in a similar way to acupuncture. Once again, as with other emergency equipment, a first aid kit is not on board just for show; it can have a vital role to play. This role can only be effective if you are familiar with the contents of the kit, and have some knowledge of first aid. If you ever use anything from the kit make sure that it is replaced when you are next in harbour. If it hasn't been used for some while do not let the first aid kit fester in some remote stowage spot on board – keep it handy, ready for use where it will also be checked regularly.

BILGE PUMPS

Bilge pumps are another vital piece of equipment, both to remove any water which might collect in the bottom of the boat and to give you some chance of keeping the flow under control in the event of a severe leak. It is often said that a frightened man with a bucket is one of the most effective bilge pumps, but one of the problems with a bucket is actually getting to the water to be able to bail it out. Properly installed bilge pumps can get right to the heart of the matter and provide a much more effective solution.

Bilge pumps come in three types; hand, electric and main engine operated. Main engine belt driven pumps are less common these days since the introduction of the simple and reliable electric bilge pump which is a self-contained unit. An engine driven pump has a certain merit, but it needs a clutch in the system to isolate the pump and the belt drive when the pump is not in use because this type of pump (with a rubber impeller) does not like running dry. Perhaps the biggest disadvantage with this type of pump is that in an emergency, when you really need the pump to work, the main engine could be out of operation.

Electric Bilge Pumps
Electric bilge pumps are ideal for routine pumping of the bilges. If the boat is divided into watertight compartments a separate pump is needed for each, although on some boats the watertight bulkhead is pierced by a short pipe with a valve which can be opened to let water drain aft so that only one pump is needed to serve the whole boat. On planing boats the electric pump should be located far aft because this is the deepest part of the boat, whilst on displacement boats the optimum place is probably in the skeg.

In normal circumstances very little water will find its way into the bilges and the only source of water is likely to be either spillage in the accommodation or a slight leak through the stern gland. Only a small pump is needed to handle this. An electric bilge pump can be fitted which has an automatic float switch which will switch on the pump when the water level rises above a prescribed height and switch the pump off again when the water level has fallen. Float switches are useful if you leave the boat unattended for any time. To operate effectively in this role the bilge pump has to be wired directly to the battery so that it will bypass the battery isolating switch. If you do this you must take particular care with the wiring so that you do not end up with a flat battery when you come back on board. Electric bilge pumps fitted with a float switch usually have a two-way switch at the dashboard, which allows them to be put into either manual or automatic operation. At sea it makes sense to keep the switch in the manual position so that occasionally you will have to go down and check the bilges, which should be part of your seagoing routine.

Hand Bilge Pumps
Electrical systems are never 100 per cent reliable and could fail just when you need them in an emergency. This is why you should always have a manual bilge pump on board, which really is your last resort in terms of removing water from the boat. Any manual bilge pump of this type should be a high capacity unit capable of shifting quite large quantities of water so that if an engine water inlet pipe fails you at least have some chance of keeping the water inflow under control until you can get to the seacock or jam something in the hole. If the boat has a common bilge one pump is adequate, or you may have two separate suction pipes to different compartments leading to the one pump, with a valve system to switch from one to the other. Modern manual pumps of this type can handle a surprising amount of water and even a certain amount of solid debris. For this reason good size suction pipes help the flow. In a dire emergency you might have to use the pump for an hour or two to keep the boat afloat, so having the pump in a place where it can be used easily could mean the difference between success and failure. So give the pump the priority it deserves.

The critical part of any bilge pumping system is the suction in the bilges. Anything floating around down there will be attracted to the suction pipes like a magnet – you can be sure the pump will block just at the most inconvenient time. The remedy, of course, is not to have anything in the bilges capable of blocking the pump, but in an emergency all sorts of bits and pieces may come adrift and end up there. One remedy is to fit a strum box on the end of the bilge suction tube so that there is less chance of it getting blocked by debris, but even strum boxes can get clogged fairly easily. The best solution is to have the bilge suction easily accessible so that you can get to it when it is blocked. This applies to both the electric and the manual pumping systems. It is better to have the pump in an accessible position even if this is not always the lowest part of the boat because a blocked pump is just as bad as having no pump at all.

BURGLAR ALARMS

One of the sad things about boating today is that motor cruisers are almost more vulnerable in harbour than they are at sea. In harbour the risk is from 'light-fingered' people, and whilst it is possible to lock your boat up, this is really no deterrent to the determined thief. Whilst marinas may offer a degree of security, some form of burglar alarm system can be very useful.

The main cabin door is likely to be the point of entry for burglars because they can work on this door relatively unseen. Burglar sensors can take the form of pressure pads under mats, infra-red beams across the entrance point or heat sensors which detect the presence of a human being. The choice of sensor will depend on the layout of the boat. The heat sensor is probably the most sophisticated, although you may have problems with this if you want to put it on while the boat's engines are still hot after you have come in from the sea.

Whatever type of sensor you have it could be linked to a siren or similar loud device which, in theory, is enough to frighten off a burglar. More sophisticated systems can be linked into the marina office so that the police can be summoned to deal with the problem. An alerting system such as this can also be used for fire and bilge water level monitoring, and with such a system you have a comprehensive security coverage when your boat is left unattended, which should give you peace of mind during the long winter nights.

TOOLS AND SPARES

In keeping with the philosophy that you ought to be self-sufficient as far as possible when at sea, it is essential to have a good selection of tools and spares on board so that you can effect at least a temporary repair to get you home if things go wrong. It is almost impossible to carry tools and spares to cope with every eventuality, so the best idea is to carry equipment of a general rather than a specific nature.

The engine is the obvious place where you will have to carry out repair work and a good set of spanners and screwdrivers is essential. Don't forget suitable spanners for the stern gland and check if there are any large or awkward nuts which you may have to cope with. A good adjustable spanner is always a useful addition to the tool kit. A few basic woodworking tools are also useful to have on board and these should be suitable for use with fibreglass as well. A drill, saw and a hammer are the basics required to enable you to carry out temporary repairs, but you might like to supplement these with a variety of other tools if you are an owner who likes to add fixtures and fittings to the boat.

As regards spares, Murphy's law will almost certainly dictate that you don't have the right spare on board when something goes wrong! With regard to the engine, spare driving belts, water pump or impeller and sparking plugs are basics, but you should supplement these with a variety of bits and pieces such as lengths of hose, worm drive clips, nuts and bolts and a selection of sealing materials for different applications. There are some wonderful sealing tapes of different types on the market today which can be used for temporary repairs. Your aim should be to have something to cope with almost any situation which arises. To work this out you need to look carefully around the boat, work out what might go wrong, such as a leaking fuel tank or a split water hose, and then decide how you might effect a temporary repair, making a list of the bits and pieces that you might need.

As far as electrical equipment is concerned, you must have at least one spare fuse for every fuse on board. It pays to have these carefully labelled so that you don't have to search around in the dark to find the right one. There is probably not a lot you can do with electronic equipment if it goes wrong, short of replacing a fuse, but so often the fault is in the electrical circuit supplying the system. Spare wires with clip fittings can often be used to bypass the main circuits to get things working again.

One of the problems which may cause you trouble at sea is equipment coming adrift. Useful things to carry in your spares bag are odd lengths of rope and elastic cord. Webbing straps can be very useful, particularly if they have the type of tensioning devices used for securing lorry loads attached to the ends. In a real emergency such as a broken engine mounting or similar disaster you might be able to use them to hold the engine temporarily in place as a 'get you home' device.

Coping with emergencies of all types at sea requires considerable ingenuity in order to find a solution. The chances of making a permanent repair may be remote but all you are really looking for is the means of effecting some sort of temporary repair which will enable you to make your way back into harbour where you can put the boat into the hands of an expert. Out at sea you are very much on your own. A good tool kit and spares bag can save you a great deal of embarrassment in having to call for help or (even worse) having to use some of the other equipment mentioned in this chapter which is there for emergencies only.

12 · Understanding the weather

The weather has a profound influence on everything you do in a motor cruiser. The world always looks a better place when the sun is shining and nowhere is this more true than when you are out at sea. By contrast, rain can make life damp and unpleasant even in a fully enclosed motor cruiser but it is the wind which must be your prime concern. The interaction between the wind and surface of the sea causes waves and it is waves which cause most of the problems that boats encounter. Any boat going to sea must live in harmony with the weather as it will dictate most of your actions and so an understanding of the weather, how it develops and its influence on the sea is important, not only to get the best out of your motor cruising but also to operate your boat safely.

In these days of efficient weather forecasts, it could be argued that there is no real need to understand the weather and what causes it; all you have to do is tune in to the weather forecast to find out what weather is predicted and then make your decisions accordingly. That would be fine if weather forecasts covered every local area and every possibility but even then no detail is given about the effect of the wind on the sea. Weather forecasts merely give you a general picture of the weather situation and what is happening; from that point on it is up to you as an individual concerned with a particular boat and a particular area of the coast to interpret those weather patterns, relate them to what you see going on around you and make your decisions accordingly.

Contrary to general belief, weather forecasts are generally very accurate in terms of the type of weather which they predict.

Where they can, fall down is on the timing of changes in the weather. Often the conditions which are forecast are already in evidence or else they may take a considerable time to arrive. It is relatively easy to forecast the *type* of weather which is going to occur but it is much more difficult to say *when* changes will occur, particularly when the forecast is based on information which may be several hours old. It is because of this difficulty in timing that a synopsis or a verbal picture of the general weather pattern is included in many forecasts. This gives the positions and expected movements of the areas of high and low pressure and their associated frontal systems. Once you have this information and know the characteristic weather associated with the passage of the various fronts and depressions, you can then relate the predicted conditions to what is actually happening around you and forecast the weather more accurately.

It is not only in improving the accuracy in terms of timing of the weather forecast that an understanding of the weather helps but also in anticipating what might be happening in the future. In particular, you need to know about any changes in the wind direction and strength because these can affect your strategy. You may currently be in sheltered water with the wind blowing off the land but a change in the wind direction could very quickly make this an exposed coast with the sea building up rapidly and harbour entrances becoming difficult. This is the sort of situation which is quite easy to predict if you listen to the weather forecasts and keep an eye open for what the weather around you is doing. You will then become aware of the changes as they occur and be able to keep one jump ahead of the weather.

Presentation of weather forecasts can differ greatly in different parts of the world. In some places the seaman has to make do with the land weather forecasts and try to relate them to the adjacent sea conditions. In other areas there are specialised shipping forcasts, but here the area of coverage tends to be general rather than specific. The best bet for the motor cruiser owner is the specialised forecast for yachtsmen issued by many local radio stations which tends to home in much more on local conditions, with particular reference to the sea conditions. These are the three general types of forecast broadcast by radio and television, but you can often supplement these by forecasts obtained by telephone from local met offices, which help to build up a picture of what is going on in the atmosphere.

It is not unusual to find an air of pessimism in many of the specialised yachting forecasts and the wind strengths quoted tend to be the maximum which might be expected over, say, a 12 hour period, so that in effect you could find conditions at sea much better than you expected from the forecast. However, forecasters have to play it safe in this respect and they get no thanks if they entice you out to sea with a good forecast and then you find that the conditions are much worse than you expected. At the end of the day, you have to accept that a weather forecast is only a guide and it is up to you as skipper to make your own final judgements.

You can learn a lot by going onto the harbour wall and looking to see what conditions are like outside, but again you have to remember that the wind inshore (where it is slowed down by the land) may not be as strong as the wind further out. This will give you a 'feel' for the weather, however, and if you have any doubts about the conditions then you should stay in harbour.

THE WEATHER PATTERN

The weather is generated by a series of high and low pressure areas around the world, and it is the interaction of these varying pressure areas and their associated fronts and troughs that dictate what the weather will be. Depressions, in particular, tend to bring bad weather conditions, whilst in general high pressure areas with their gentle isobars bring fine weather and sunny conditions. This is a very broad generalisation, however, and the interaction between the high and low pressures need to be carefully judged in order to build up a picture of the overall conditions. Within this pattern it is the fronts moving through which bring about changes, particularly in wind strength and direction.

A *depression* is an area of low atmospheric pressure around which the wind revolves in an anti-clockwise direction, spiralling in towards the centre. Thus, if the centre of the depression is to the north of the observer, the wind should be westerly, but the spiralling effect will tend to make the wind a little south of west. Buys Ballot's law states that when you are standing with your back to the wind the lower pressure (i.e. the

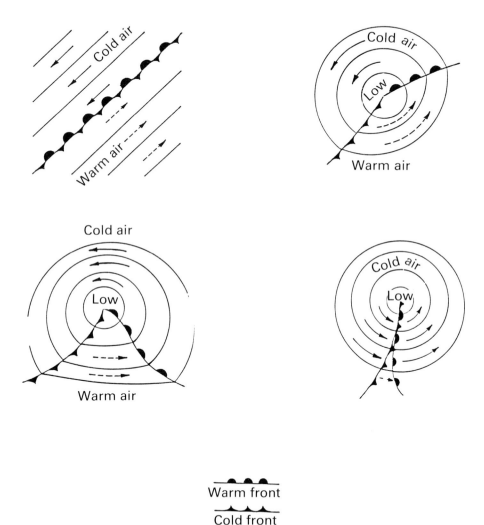

Warm front

Cold front

Occluded front

The development of a typical depression in the northern hemisphere.

centre of the depression) will always be on your left (this is reversed in the southern hemisphere). Using this law can help you in your weather forecasting.

In *high pressure* areas the wind revolves around the centre of high pressure in the opposite direction, i.e. clockwise. Whereas a low pressure area is complicated by frontal systems, high pressure areas tend to be much more docile and do not have any associated fronts.

Frontal Systems
A front is the borderline between warm and cold air masses. Depressions are initially formed along the boundary area between the two air masses. The term 'front' is reminiscent of a battlefield, and to some extent this is what a weather front is, with the warm air and the cold air 'fighting' and making incursions into each other's territory.

A large frontal system extends right round the northern hemisphere, this being the junction between the cold polar air and the warmer air to the south. The winds on each side of this front flow in nearly opposite directions. It is the turbulence between these two air masses that bends the front into an eddy, which in turn can develop into the circular flow of a depression. The fronts continue as a feature of the depression, forming the active parts of that depression. Two fronts are formed, one where the warm air is rising over the cold air on the leading side of the depression and the other where the cold air is forcing its way under the warm air on the trailing side of the depression. The first type, where the warm air is overtaking the cold, is called a warm front and the second, where the cold air is overtaking the warm, is called a cold front. The diagrams opposite should make these features clearer.

A cold front will tend to move more quickly than a warm front because in the former the cold overtaking air is moving along the surface. In a warm front the warm overtaking air has to 'climb over' the cold air and is slowed by this gradient. As the depression develops the cold front will gradually catch up with the warm front and this usually happens near the centre of the depression first, where the fronts have less distance to travel. When the two fronts combine in this way it then becomes known

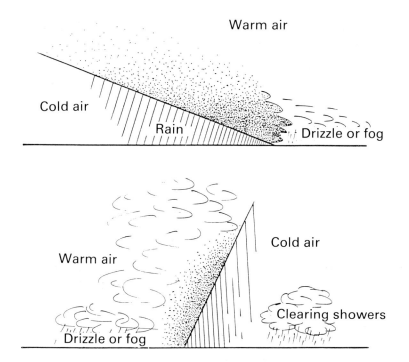

*Cross-section of a cold front (top) and warm front (bottom),
showing the type of weather which might be expected as the front
goes through.*

as an *occluded* front. The formation of an occluded front is
usually an indication that the depression is weakening.

Fronts are important features because they are the most
active areas of a depression and are also the regions where
changes in wind strength and direction occur. These changes
happen with all fronts but are usually more pronounced on a
cold front, where the wind direction could change as much as 90
degrees as the front passes through a fixed point. To the motor
cruiser crew, such a change of wind direction can be of major
significance; if you can recognise the features of a front you will
be able to predict the changes in the wind and weather.

Warm Fronts
The approach of a warm front can be gauged by a steady lowering
of cloud height, which starts off as high, thin cloud and

gradually becomes thicker, heavier and lower. As cloud thickens, rain – probably just a light drizzle to start with – will start falling, perhaps 200 miles in front of the actual frontal line. As the cloud gets lower and heavier the rain will become heavier and more persistent, indicating the approach of a warm front. Thunderstorms may occur in this area, particularly during the summer when the air is likely to be more unstable. If the front is weak there may be little or no rain, but in such a weak front there is unlikely to be much wind either.

By the time the front itself appproaches you can expect heavy, low cloud with wet, murky weather. As the front passes through the rain will stop and brighter weather can be expected. There may be a noticeable rise in temperature after the front has passed and as the effect of the warm air behind the front begins to be felt. As the front passes through the wind will veer (swing in a clockwise direction) and will probably blow just as hard or even increase a little. With a warm front a dramatic alteration in wind direction is not likely but you cannot expect any reduction in the wind strength.

Cold Fronts
In contrast to a warm front, a cold front is much less predictable and can take various forms. Instead of the gradual build-up and change associated with the approach of a warm front, a cold front may announce its arrival by strong squalls of both wind and rain and by heavy, towering clouds. The front itself is usually the most active part of the change, the point where the cold air is pushing under the warm air and creating turbulence. In some types of cold front line squalls form, which can generate very heavy rain and quite strong local winds. As the cold front passes, the heavy rain associated with the surface front will gradually die out and higher clouds, with eventually clear skies, will follow. There may still be isolated showers, but in general the weather takes on the characteristic bright, rather hard looking sky of the calm after the storm. Although the wind may still be blowing hard at this stage, the passage of the cold front usually indicates that the worst of the depression is past.

Occluded Fronts

When the faster moving cold front catches up with the warm front, the fronts become occluded. Here you can expect heavy, continuous rain, a feature of occluded fronts. These fronts are usually slow moving so that the rain is persistent, but you have the consolation that such a feature indicates that the depression itself is weakening and there is unlikely to be any major change in wind direction.

Secondary Depressions

The fronts which are such a feature of depressions are generally only found on the equatorial side of depressions and rarely on the polar side. If the centre of the depression passes to the north of you in the northern hemisphere you must expect the activity and changing conditions generated by fronts. If the depression passes to the south the weather will generally be much more settled with steady changes in wind direction as the depression moves past, although more active weather changes will be noticeable if you are close to the centre of the depression.

Forecasters track depressions very closely and experience has enabled them to predict their path with a degree of certainty. This means that weather forecasts are generally reliable when depressions and high pressure areas are behaving according to the prescribed pattern, but occasionaly the unpredictable happens and this is often associated with the development of a secondary depression along one of the fronts.

Secondary depressions are usually associated with a very active cold front. They are more common in the summer months when local variations in temperature can provide the additional energy to start the circulation of a secondary depression. They can develop very quickly, and can become very intense. The indication of such a depression would initially be a fairly rapid and unexpected drop in the barometer reading, together with an increase in the wind and an unpredicted change in wind direction. However, these depressions are fast moving and by the time you are aware of the situation it is likely that the wind will be making sea conditions hazardous anyway and the time to head for home will be long overdue.

This example of how weather conditions can change suddenly is given mainly to advise you not to rely too much on weather forecasts. If you do, sooner or later it will get you into trouble. You should always relate the weather to the conditions around you. Both before you go to sea, but more importantly when you are at sea, be aware of the conditions, check the wind direction and strength at regular intervals and watch the sky for changes in cloud formations. There are lots of signs around you to show what the weather is doing and how it is changing; if you marry these to the forecast you will not only have much better appreciation of how the weather is developing, but you will also feel much more in control of the situation.

RELATING THE WIND TO THE SEA CONDITIONS

A strong wind on its own will not do you much harm, although it can make handling the boat in harbour quite tricky. What you are really concerned with is the effect of the wind on the sea conditions in harbour entrances and open water and this is where you have to develop your own skills of interpretation. If there were no tides or currents and if the sea were a uniform depth the sea conditions would be very predictable. You would know that if the wind was blowing Force 5 you would have an uncomfortable sea with the tops of the waves just starting to break and you would certainly know that if it reached Force 6 or 7 it would be time to head for home, or if in harbour, to stay put. These are the easy situations to forecast but the wind is only one of the many influences acting on the surface of the sea. When wind, tide and perhaps shallow water all take effect, sea conditions can occur out of proportion to the wind generating them. It is these, often local, conditions which can cause danger.

Wind, Tide and Currents
Strong tides and currents occur in many parts of the world, particularly around coastlines. Coastlines are rarely regular so when the tidal flow is distorted by having to pass around headlands or over shallow rocks, the water flow becomes disturbed. Even on a calm day the turbulence in the water can be seen by the breaking wave formation. If you add the wind to this

unhealthy mixture quite turbulent seas can result, often fairly local in extent. It is not too difficult to predict where and how these more difficult sea conditions might occur so that you can take steps to avoid them.

The two main sets of sea conditions which will affect your motor cruiser are those when the wind is against the tide and when the wind is with the tide (see Chapter 4). When there is no tide or current the wind generates waves, the height of which is dependent on the strength of the wind. The higher the waves, the greater the wavelength, i.e. the distance between one wave crest and the next. This means that whatever the height of the wave, the gradient (the slope of the wave) remains much the same. In normal conditions this gradient is such that you can drive your motor cruiser over it quite comfortably, provided you adapt your speed to the conditions.

As the wind strength increases the gradient on the lee side of the wave tends to become steeper; it can steepen to the point where the wave is unstable and starts to break. You see this first in winds of about Force 4 or 5 where the wind pressure on the crest of the wave helps to make the wave unstable and what are known as 'white horses' start to appear. These are not dangerous to the average motor cruiser because it is only the tip of the wave breaking. However, these 'white horses' serve as a warning that the wind is rising and you ought to consider your position. If the wind continues to rise to Force 6 the pressure of the wind on the back of the wave can lead to greater instability and you can find the waves starting to break along a longer crest and with more weight of water behind it; it is this moving water on the surface which can start to put you and your boat under stress.

When a tide or a current is running it means that the whole body of water is moving along. If this movement happens to be in the same direction as the wind, it has the effect of increasing the wave length and reducing the gradient of the waves so that there is less likelihood of the waves breaking. In fact, when wind and tide are moving in the same direction, even in a comparatively strong wind of say Force 6, the sea conditions can be quite moderate and you can be lulled into a false sense of security. When the tide turns there will be a marked deterioration in the conditions because wind and tide are acting in opposite directions. The wave length will effectively be shortened, increasing the gradient of the waves so that they are much more likely to break. In these conditions with a strong tide and perhaps only a Force 4 wind, you can encounter quite uncomfortable breaking seas. Fortunately with this wind strength the wave height is not likely to be high enough to cause too much anxiety. However, it is the shortening of the wave length which can make life very uncomfortable because the boat will pitch or roll a great deal more rapidly and you may get the uncomfortable feeling of the boat being out of step with the waves.

It is often hard to find a comfortable speed which matches that of the wave conditions. Before the boat has had a chance to recover from one wave it will be encountering the next, and you may begin to feel out of control of the situation.

In fresher conditions, these wind against tide seas can become positively dangerous because the breaking sea may reach you before the bow of the boat has had a chance to lift, resulting in an awful lot of water crashing on board.

Normal tides or currents do not exceed 2 knots. Under these conditions, whilst there will be a noticeable change in sea conditions between the ebb and flow of the tide, you are not likely to encounter anything positively dangerous in the normal wind strengths in which you operate your motor cruiser. However, because the tide flows through channels and around uneven coastlines, you will find local areas where the tide flows much more strongly and these are the places where you can get really nasty sea conditions when the wind is against a strong tide. You often find areas like this off headlands which are very pronounced and which jut out into the tidal stream; in extreme cases there will be a back eddy behind the headland where the tidal stream goes round in a complete circle and produces the most difficult and unpredictable sea conditions when the wind is against the tide. Most of the areas where these tide rips occur are marked on the chart; they should be treated with caution. Even in fine conditions you may be aware of the turbulence in the water and in a planing boat you should watch out for unpredictable wave formations. You can often see the broken water from some distance off, sometimes appearing as a very clear-cut and straight line on the surface of the water which divides the breaking waves from the relative calm on the other side of the line.

Crossing Waves

Another situation where difficult sea conditions can develop and where you need to drive your boat with care is when you have crossing wave patterns. The sea surface is rarely covered by a simple, undirectional wave pattern. Instead it consists of waves coming from several different directions, although there will generally be one predominant wave pattern generated by the wind blowing at the time.

If the wind suddenly changes direction, the prevailing wave pattern will not die out immediately; superimposed upon it will be a new wave pattern generated by the new wind and these crossing seas can produce some nasty pyramidal waves where the wave crests coincide. Long before this type of sea condition is generated you will probably be heading for harbour and safety but you can sometimes find this type of sea off harbours where there are vertical breakwaters and near cliffs which go vertically into the sea in comparatively deep water. With a deep ocean swell coming in and hitting such cliffs, you can feel the reflected waves over a mile offshore. In general, these are areas to avoid in such circumstances because of the difficult sea conditions generated.

Shallow Water

Shallow water also has its effect on waves. Instead of the normal pattern of waves generated by the wind which tend to extend fairly deep in the water, the shallow water forces the wave upwards and consequently increases the gradient, making the wave unstable and causing it to break. Particularly with a big swell, which may not in itself be particularly dangerous from the point of view of a motor cruiser, this phenomenon of breaking shallow water can occur even in comparatively light wind conditions and is usually found at the entrance to river harbours where there is a shallow water bar. The effect of the breaking seas will be exaggerated if an ebb tide or a current is running out

222 · AN INTRODUCTION TO POWERBOAT CRUISING

of the river meeting these waves coming in. Once again, very nasty local conditions can arise in this situation in marked contrast to the comparative calm outside.

These are all conditions that you need to learn about to fully appreciate the effect of the wind on the sea, but in most cases you can gain experience of them gently by going to sea in fine or moderate conditions and getting the feel of the waves and the way they change in different conditions. In a motor boat the waves are your playground but also your enemy and you will develop a love/hate relationship with them and the wind that forms them – a relationship which demands respect and understanding of the conditions, so that waves and boat can live in a degree of harmony to make cruising a pleasure.

POOR VISIBILITY

This chapter is beginning to sound as though it is trying to put you off motor cruising altogether, but it is really an attempt to help you understand fully the conditions in which your boat operates. It is rather like learning to drive a car in a wide variety of road conditions ranging from wet and bumpy roads in the country to straight, dry highways. Visibility can have a considerable effect on the way you drive. The same applies to a motor boat where poor visibility suddenly closes in the world around you. Poor visibility of anything less than a mile can start to affect your navigation, and if it comes down to a quarter of a mile or less then it can also be worrying as far as collision avoidance is concerned. Remember that you should always drive your boat at a speed at which enables you to stop in at least half the range of visibility. Rocks which loom out of the fog are especially nerve-wracking, and a moderate speed, directly related to the conditions, is vital to safety in poor conditions.

Rain
Both rain and fog cause poor visibility at sea. In rain it is not just the actual visibility which is a problem but also the fact that it can be further limited by the inadequacies of the windscreen wipers on the boat. Almost invariably these will only give the view ahead and you should be just as concerned about what is

happening to port and starboard of you. Conditions will be even more difficult if you have an open steering position and the speed of the boat should be adjusted accordingly.

Fog
Whilst rain can be forecast quite reliably, fog is quite another matter and probably represents one of the biggest hazards to navigation you are likely to experience. Fog is caused when warm, moist air meets something cold. This could be air, water or land, but either way the result is that you are enveloped in a damp, wet blanket of fog which can severely hamper your vision. Fog often appears around the coastline where warm air coming off the sea hits the cold land, although sometimes the opposite can occur. Fog also occurs in the warm air sector of both warm and cold fronts.

Whilst it is comparatively easy to forecast fog in a general way, its actual occurrence can be quite local in extent; patchy fog is possibly one of the worst hazards for seafarers. You can find yourself travelling at speed in bright conditions and suddenly enter a bank of fog with very little warning and very little indication of what lies inside the fog, a position which takes a little time to appreciate and which can give you a fright if you come across another boat. Because fog tends to be prevalent around coastlines where there are different land and sea temperatures, one of the worst hazards you can face is being enveloped in fog just as you are making your landfall or approaching a harbour. Radar has taken many of the risks out of encountering fog in this way; it at least enables you to navigate with a degree of safety. But without radar you are very much on your own. This is where your navigation can really be put to the test and where your prior planning and preparation will pay off.

ASSESSING THE WEATHER

Before you go to sea you must make an assessment of the weather conditions, both what it will be like when you get outside the harbour, and even more importantly what it will be like when you are approaching your destination. In checking weather forecasts you will look for changes in wind direction and strength and the prospects for rain and fog. You will want to make sure that if you have shelter from the land at the start of your passage you will not find yourself suddenly exposed to a fresh breeze when the wind changes as you proceed along your course.

The next thing to do is to check the tides from the almanac, and from the tidal atlas to find which direction the water will be flowing so that you can identify areas where the wind may be against the tide and where you can expect worse conditions. Only experience can really tell you what conditions might be like in a particular area, but knowing the strength of the wind and the tide is part of your responsibility as skipper.

Having made your assessment of the weather the logical thing to do if you have any doubts at all about the conditions is not to go. Doubt will creep in if the wind is freshening or if there is poor visibility and if you have doubts, wait for conditions to improve. However, in making these assessments and raising these doubts you have to remember that they are only based on forecasts, which tend to talk about the maximum wind strengths and the worst conditions in order to play safe. One of the best ways of testing the conditions and finding out if you are comfortable is to actually go and try it for yourself; this can be done quite simply if you have a harbour which gives you easy and safe access to the open sea. You can put your nose outside the harbour, judge the conditions and then make up your mind what to do.

If you have a long run over open water with nothing in the way of ports of refuge on the way then don't make the passage if the forecast is at all marginal. Once you are on your way you are virtually committed. However, if you are heading out along the coast and there are several ports before you reach your final destination then you could think about taking the weather one step at a time. If conditions look good once you are outside the harbour, then take as a first step the route to the next safe harbour and then make a further appraisal of the conditions. Do make sure, however, that deteriorating weather will not make conditions in the entrances to these alternative harbours difficult or dangerous. There is a lot to be said for trying this approach, i.e. getting out there and sampling the conditions for yourself. This is the way to build experience but you need to exercise caution. Provided you always keep something in hand both in terms of the sea conditions and in places where you can run for shelter, this type of passage making can be both satisfying and practical.

Of course, you may be one of those fortunate owners who do all their boating in areas where the sun always shines and the wind is gentle, in which case the weather is not something you have to exercise your mind about greatly. However, even in these conditions the unexpected can happen and you should never go to sea without at least obtaining a forecast. To the majority of owners their boating is much more sensitive to the wind and weather and with experience it becomes almost second nature to keep one eye open for weather changes, to sense the changing pattern of the waves as the wind and tide change and to adapt the speed of the boat to the conditions, always bearing in mind the need to have a safe harbour close at hand or, if not, to be very confident about the stability of the weather conditions.

Epilogue

You have come to terms with the weather, you have learned the effect of the tides and currents, and most important of all you have learned to know and understand the sea. There is a lot to learn when you take to the sea in a motor boat and yet so much of it comes down to experience. You have to get a feel for the sea, to understand it in all its moods and to balance the behaviour of your boat to that of the sea.

It is so easy, in a powerboat, to think that you are master, that you can dictate the terms when you go to sea. If you adopt that attitude you will come unstuck sooner or later. Even a powerboat has to move in harmony with the sea and work with it, not against it. This is the lesson you learn after years of experience – in the early days you are bound to make mistakes. But don't be put off by these mistakes; they are all part of the learning process. Rather, when you do make a mistake, make sure that you have some margin for error so that the consequences will not be too serious. It is only lifeboats and racing boats that have to push things to the limits; that's why they need the best boats, the best equipment and, most important of all, experience.

In your early days at sea, take things gently, make sure you have a good margin for error and then you will enjoy the pleasures of the sea. You will soon be relaxed about your boating, but all the time keeping a weather eye open for the unexpected. Out at sea, you are on your own. You have to make the decisions, you have to fix things when they go wrong. Preparation is the name of the game and I hope this book will point you in the right direction. I have spent 40 years in boats and ships of all types and still I am surprised by what the sea and the weather can have in store. In a world where so much is packaged and presented in a safe way the sea is one of the few places where you really live by your wits. That, for me, is its attraction.

Pleasant boating.

DISCARD